Developmental Disability

A Family Challenge

Sr. Mary Theodore Hegeman, O.S.F.

Paulist Press  *New York/Ramsey*

Copyright © 1984 by
Sr. Mary Theodore Hegeman, O.S.F.

All rights reserved. No part of this book may be reproduced or transmitted in any form or by any means, electronic or mechanical, including photocopying, recording or by any information storage and retrieval system without permission in writing from the Publisher.

Library of Congress
Catalog Card Number: 83-62953

ISBN: 0-8091-2615-X

Published by Paulist Press
545 Island Road, Ramsey, N.J. 07446

Printed and bound in the
United States of America

Contents

	Foreword *by Joseph Cardinal Bernardin*	1
	Preface by *Robert Perske*	3
	Author's Note	5
1.	A Starting Point	8
2.	Surveying the Problem	16
3.	Contrasting Conditions	33
4.	Uniqueness of Person	48
5.	Family Attitudes	64
6.	Reaching Toward Maturity	74
7.	Considering Sexuality	83
8.	Crisis Situations	104
9.	Conflict with the Law	115
10.	In Touch with God	128
11.	Historical Survey	145
12.	Breakthroughs	161
	Annotated and Youth Bibliographies	182, 191

To
Saint Joseph:
Advocate for all Persons
with Special Needs

Foreword

Parents and relatives of developmentally disabled children will certainly appreciate this work by Sister Mary Theodore Hegeman, O.S.F. Her wisdom is well expressed in *Developmental Disability: A Family Challenge.*

In the first six chapters, Sister Mary Theodore presents a clear picture of the developmental challenges with which the disabled child must cope and the impact each phase has on the family or the residential community. The significance of various disabilities is explored so that family attitudes can strike a balance between despair and unrealistic expectations.

The phases of development that are experienced especially on the threshold of adulthood and throughout adulthood are carefully examined. Sister Mary Theodore expresses particular concern that adults who are developmentally disabled be given not only the credit they deserve as adults, but also the support they need as they make their way through life.

In the *Document of the Holy See for the International Year of Disabled Persons* (March 4, 1981), we read: "Since the person suffering from handicaps is a subject with full rights, he or she must be helped to take his or her place in society in all aspects and at all levels as far as is compatible with his or her capabilities." The significant question is not whether the person is brain-damaged, a victim of an accident or genetic problems. The significant issue centers on whether the individual is a person with a personality unique in the world. The person who is developmentally disabled has the *right* to a place in the world and a *right* to make his or her contribution.

Sister Mary Theodore treats in a down-to-earth fashion the very real and practical concerns of sexuality, the effects of sickness or loss of loved ones on the life of the developmentally disabled person, and the problems that arise when behavior is in conflict with law. Her treatment of crisis situations will prove a valuable resource for family members and those in the helping professions who are called upon to give support.

In the final chapters the reader is taken through the past into the future. Though the past often makes dismal reading, the future is brighter because of the pioneering work done with perseverance and hope by Sister Mary Theodore and her Community at St. Coletta School.

Joseph Cardinal Bernardin

Preface

I can recall, in 1961, searching the stacks of six university libraries for significant books on mental retardation. It didn't take long since the books never took up more than five feet of shelf space. I nevertheless found Sister Mary Theodore's *The Challenge of the Retarded Child* in each library I visited.

Hers was one of the few books in that period that dared its readers to *value* these persons with handicaps. Most of the others emphasized negative things about these persons—their oddities, the terrible sufferings their parents were expected to endure, the hobbling effect they had on our pursuit for national perfection, and detailed programs for "managing" them in out-of-the-way places. But this sister, influenced by her faith, gave the world two things: she gave her understanding of the major documents of the day as seen through her eyes and she shared her experiences with "living documents" with whom she worked (those seeking her kindness, her accepting hugs, her help in doing things they never did before, and her assurance that they could help make the world a better place, too). It was her restatement of issues, backed by vignettes about real people, that helped many earlier clinicians and volunteers discover previously unseen doors in our field.

Today, university libraries are filled with books—hundreds of books—on persons with developmental disabilities (a more recent term for these people). But there remains the need for a book with the human touch of Sister Mary Theodore.

Fortunately, she has fulfilled this need. In this freshly written book, she shows that while we have been growing in our attitudes toward people with disabilities, so has she.

In her inimitable way, she faces the issues of the 1980's head-on. One of the most important ideas in the book: she refuses to see persons with disabilities as eternal children. Instead, she demonstrates on page after page the need to plan for their adulthood. As usual, she describes current breakthroughs in the field as seen through her eyes.

Sister Mary Theodore cannot be typed and categorized as a disciple of any single school of thought. You may disagree with her at times, and yet one thing is certain. She forces you to rethink your position with regard to major issues in the field today. Books like this raise our consciousness and make us grow.

Robert Perske
(Author of *New Life in the Neighborhood*
and *Hope for the Families*)

Author's Note

The focus of this sequel to *The Challenge of the Retarded Child* is on adults who are developmentally disabled. However, the preparation for adulthood grows through the experiences of childhood and adolescence. The whole life span needs direction so that the child who is different will be less different as an adult.

Including basic information from my earlier book, the present study of developmental disability presents a challenge which begins in earliest infancy and reaches its climax in the adult. New alternatives are opening for people who are handicapped. They are beginning to have choice and control in their own life situations. In this book, some of them speak for themselves. Expectancy must be expanded from the self-fulfilling restrictive prophecies of the past to provide the most enabling opportunities and environment reaching into the future.

The terms *developmental disability, mental handicap,* and *mental retardation* are used interchangeably, although technically they are not synonymous. Concern here is for the individual so affected as a person and the impact on the family, the basic unit of society.

In the more than fifty years that my life has been involved with that of people who are handicapped, and with their family members, there have been continuous changes. From the early 1930's institutions and Opportunity Rooms stand out clearly in my memory. I recall visiting institutions where herding large numbers of helpless people into crowded dayrooms and dormitories was the general pattern. Some situations were appalling, but I would admire the staff who could offer care, day after day, in such adverse circumstances. I remember hearing a national leader say, "Those huge institutions should be bulldozed over," and the gradual trend toward deinstitutionalization began to develop.

In the special classes, or Opportunity Rooms, the happiness philosophy prevailed. In fact, examples linger with me of instances where pupils in the regular classes envied the fun that special students had. This subconscious envy may have been reflected in name-calling and ridicule. Differences and deficiencies, rather than normal traits and individual abilities, seemed to attract attention. With the passage of years there has been a growing trend toward developing the person who is retarded to full potential, with growth toward social adjustment, self-support, and finding a place in the stream of life.

The success of these efforts has depended greatly upon the economic conditions of the time. When employment opportunities were favorable, persons with handicaps could get satisfying jobs and hold them through the years. With high unemployment, they must often be content with the least desirable working conditions, or no job at all.

Those persons with developmental disability who have favorable family situations are fortunate. If well accepted at home, with a niche in the family farm or business, they can be self-supporting and have companionship. I know of others, such as Jerry, who had enough personal drive so that he could hold a job and improve his situation without family support. Jerry is among those former St. Coletta students who kept in touch for guidance and continued his education after he left the school.

Former students, such as Jerry, now adults, have been a motivating influence while this manuscript was in process. Each topic, each chapter, could be a book in itself if fully developed. Purposely I have avoided the use of footnotes, but have included an annotated bibliography to indicate sources of material and to suggest further reading.

There are many persons whom I wish to thank for their encouragement and support, beginning with the Sisters of St. Francis of Assisi and the members of my own family. To Sister Elaine Weber, administrator at St. Coletta School, and Sister Beatrice Smith, assistant in public relations services, I am indebted for an arrangement that made it possible for me to concentrate on this time-consuming work of love; and to Sister Justa Becker, librarian, for locating sources of information. For critical reading and valued suggestions I am grateful to Sister Coletta Dunn, Sister Sheila Haskett, Sister Kenan Rebholz and Mr. Fred Whitemarsh.

For the Foreword and Preface I am indebted to Joseph Cardinal Bernardin and to Mr. Robert Perske. I wish to thank Sister Joanne Marie Kliebhan, Sister Grace Schauf, Sister Mary Jeanne Quinlivan, Mrs. John Feeks, Mrs. Clyde Kieffer, Mrs. Charles Wing, Brother Charles Burns, Mr. John Melcher and Mr. Harvey Stevens for sharing information with me; also former students Roberta French, Renee (Borman) Greiner, George Kremp, James Meier and Kevin Tracy for their personal contributions. Finally, to all who contributed directly or indirectly, and to St. Coletta residents for the inspiration that prompted my work, I express my thanks. To Karen Maron I am especially grateful for her typing of the manuscript, and to Jean Marie Hiesberger for editorial guidance.

If this book helps to promote the well-being of persons who are developmentally disabled, I shall be grateful to God for having blessed our joint efforts.

Sister Mary Theodore Hegeman, O.S.F

1   *A Starting Point*

After more than fifty years of working with children and adults who have developmental disabilities, there is a special insight that I would like to share: the more these persons are given a chance to do, the more they will show they are able to accomplish. Although this truth has obvious limitations, the recognition of it has a remarkable effect on the lives of children with mental retardation and reaches into their adulthood.

When my first train ride in late August of 1926 brought me from St. Francis Convent in Milwaukee to the St. Coletta School at Jefferson, Wisconsin, I found myself in a unique situation. My teaching assignment was with primary grades in the St. Lawrence parochial school. My home was at the residential school for children and adults who are developmentally disabled. At that time a sign at the entrance read, "St. Coletta School for Backward Children." Later some of the residents protested that they don't walk backward. "St. Coletta School for Exceptional Children" emerged when the school, originally incorporated in 1913, assumed the new title in 1931.

Living on the same campus with handicapped people, my introduction to mental retardation was neither as abrupt nor as emotionally involved as that of parents who become aware that their child will never develop to the expected normal level. At the time I was content to be teaching grades one to four in the school on the hill. Between scheduled hours I developed an ever increasing interest in the work of our Sisters of St. Francis of Assisi at St. Coletta School at the foot of the hill.

These Sisters pioneered in a work that has remained unique in the religious community of which I am a member. Young and naive at the time, I wanted to be a part of their efforts to help individuals whose gifts are less than those of the average person.

Although it is not the purpose of this book to tell the story of St. Coletta School, a few historical mileposts may lead to a better understanding of the approach taken at this oldest and largest school operated by a religious community for mentally handicapped children and adults. The farm on which the main buildings are located was purchased in 1864 and the original home became the motherhouse of the Sisters of St. Francis of Assisi. In 1878 the Community returned to St. Francis Convent in Milwaukee, leaving a staff of Sisters at St. Coletta's to open a boarding school for girls of high school age. When the enrollment outgrew the facilities, transfer was made to a new building in Milwaukee, St. Mary's Academy, and St. Coletta's was available for another venture.

Success with two retarded girls who had been admitted to the academy for the sake of religious instruction had aroused the interest of the St. Coletta chaplain, Reverend George Meyer. On a trip to Tennessee in 1904 he met a family with a handicapped child. The parents asked, "Father, why doesn't the Church have a school for children like ours?"

Father Meyer regarded their daughter, a pretty little brain-injured girl, for a moment and then replied, "I will see what can be done for you."

The chaplain returned to Milwaukee where he pleaded with Mother Mary Thecla, superior of the Sisters of St. Francis at that time, to open a school for children who are mentally handicapped. On a later occasion he spoke directly to the Sisters, explaining that while it is a noble work to educate the mentally alert, it is a greater challenge to awaken dormant minds and bring them to the light of knowledge and to the love of God.

Mother Mary Thecla had agreed that if the Sisters were willing she would open a school. To her surprise, and that of Father Meyer, every Sister of the Community volunteered for this work. In an attempt to promote the undertaking, Father Meyer visited state institutions to acquaint himself with current methods and found that the care given was mainly custodial.

With four Sisters to care for the ten children initially enrolled, the St. Coletta Institute for Backward Youth was opened on September 10, 1904. Emphasis during the early years was on the provision of home care, physical comforts, spiritual assistance and minimal learning skills. Education for handicapped children in the basic school subjects was practically unknown at the turn of the century. Sister Anastasia Mueller and Sister Madeline Heimann, administrators at St. Coletta's from 1925 to 1964, gradually developed a modified program of education. Both these Sisters had the opportunity to add to their personal preparation by study at the Vineland Training School in New Jersey. Pioneering in special education, they met with opposition and even scorn, and came to know all the difficulties that accompany progress and achievement.

In 1927 the erection of a separate school building, large and modern, was a decisive step forward. Now the children could actually "go to school" as their brothers and sisters did. Only those closely associated with a handicapped person can realize how much a school program, geared to the interest level, the needs, and the abilities of the retarded, contributes to childhood happiness.

Although St. Coletta School has increased its enrollment far beyond early expectations, this growth has been aided by a continuous building and remodeling program. In order to sustain happy, friendly relations between staff members and residents in a homelike atmosphere, it is necessary to keep within the optimum capacity.

My knowledge of mental retardation and the developmental conditions involved was minimal. Vague preconceptions I then had were, in a sense, disguised blessings. Countless times they have reappeared in conversations with concerned parents. My own early experience enabled me to recognize their difficulties with greater empathy and understanding.

At first little things attracted me to the children with developmental disabilities as I grew to know them at St. Coletta School. The atmosphere of happiness they created, the welcome they gave whenever I came among them, the friendliness between staff members and children—these little things seemed momentous because they gave St. Coletta's its climate. I was impressed, too, by observing that our Franciscan Community had selected teachers who were especially devoted to this work for children with special needs.

One day I had the opportunity to act as substitute teacher and found that I liked the individual approach. My attempt to give each child the needed help according to mental ability and achievement level proved to be an exciting challenge. I wanted to join in the work. My interest in normal children had not diminished but I knew that teachers were available to guide their progress. Children with mental retardation need special help. These are the ones, a growing conviction assured me, who would call forth the best abilities I had to offer.

During the four years I lived at St. Coletta's, while teaching at St. Lawrence School, I learned from the two hundred and fifty boys and girls then enrolled at St. Coletta's that they are human individuals, each one eager to go forward at his own rate if given the opportunity. I had learned that a large percentage of mental retardation is caused by physical accident to the child. With this knowledge came a gradual realization that what had happened to these children at St. Coletta's could have happened to my own brothers and sisters or to me. It hadn't, so I was eager to devote my whole life to the care of children with mental retardation to thank God that my parents had been blessed with a family of healthy sons and daughters. I wanted to help those parents who had to face the uncertainties of raising children about whom so little was known at that time, in gratitude that my own parents were spared.

This gratitude as I volunteered led me toward a lifetime of service to developmentally disabled children, with special concern for the parents. I have known their pain keenly registered in often repeated questions:

"What is mental retardation?"
"Why is my child mentally retarded?"
"What causes this baffling condition?"
"How many children are so affected?"
"Is there a cure? What can I do for this child?"
"Where, or to whom, can I turn for help?"
"What does the future hold for this little individual who, at maturity, will continue in many ways to function as a child?"
"What purpose do these children have in life?"

More recently the term used is developmental disability, but the questions remain much the same. Although awareness of mental handicap has increased, similar questions are asked by bewildered, fearful parents when their own child shows lack of the expected development. For some of these problems there are no complete solutions, but experience has something to offer.

The purpose of my earlier book, *The Challenge of the Retarded Child,* was to develop a better understanding of children with mental retardation. Now I see the child with developmental disabilities as offering a springboard to assessing adult handicaps. Early intervention modifies adult adjustment and leads to a higher level of maturation. The role of the child presages the person who will emerge. Years of impressionable childhood pass quickly, with urgency for the best basic preparation to insure later achievement.

I have seen the value of early stimulation for Down's syndrome children in little ones who had their start at the St. Francis Children's Activity and Achievement Center, Cardinal Stritch College, Milwaukee. When these children transferred to St. Coletta School they were outstanding in language development, motor coordination, and reading readiness skills. Development of personality was striking. When little Anne would recognize something as inconsistent, and say "That is ridiculous," even grown-ups would think twice before making comments to her. Early intervention for children who are developmentally disabled will receive further attention in a later chapter.

Parents, and those who can be helpful to these parents and their developmentally disabled children, comprise the audience this book is intended to reach. Among these are the physicians, pastors, teachers, nurses, and social workers to whom parents most readily turn for help.

In sharing years of experience at St. Coletta School, I would like to indicate clearly how religion can give courage to parents of children who are mentally handicapped and motivate them to do their best for each child. Incidents and examples used in the book are drawn, for the most part, from daily life at St. Coletta's but privacy of individuals is respected.

Starting in 1904, with St. Coletta School now in the fourth quarter of a century, there have been countless opportunities to give service to individuals with special needs. Expanding study and research continue to supply information about their capacities to learn, their training, and their hope for acceptance into society. Only those closely associated with a child who finds learning difficult can realize how much a school program, geared to the interest level, the needs and the abilities of the individual, contributes to childhood happiness and to a sense of self-worth during adolescent years. A sound early foundation strengthens the self-concept and will help the different adult to feel less different.

Building a positive self-concept during early years reaches its greatest value in adulthood. The developmentally disabled person needs self-confidence in order to hold a meaningful job. This success, in turn, strengthens the self-concept. Since leisure hours are critical for the employed adult, the companionship of friends finds an important role in enriching free time. Enjoyable sharing in social experiences not only depends upon a favorable self-concept but also leads to a way of life that has dignity and fulfillment.

Since we regard our work at St. Coletta School as permanent, with consistent planning and encouragement for continuity of personnel, we have been able to gain a functional knowledge of the progress that can be achieved by developmentally disabled persons. Also, close relationship over a period of years creates a personal, family-like atmosphere. One of the glories of America today is the rising interest in aiding handicapped persons. To them, and to their parents and family members, we offer the knowledge and hope that we have grown to cherish at St. Coletta School with the assurance that they are not alone nor forgotten.

The following statement summarizes the present philosophy of St. Coletta School:

> Recognizing the human dignity and spiritual worth of persons with mental retardation, St. Coletta School attempts to provide them with quality programs of resi-

dential care, special attention, vocational habilitation, transitional group living, sheltered employment, and continuing adult development and growth. In a climate of acceptance and respect, children and young adults enrolled here are prepared for as an independent and productive adulthood as they are capable of attaining.

All persons are created by God to fulfill a unique mission on this earth, to bring into the lives of all they touch special gifts. Our goal at St. Coletta School is to prepare our students for their special mission, and it is our privilege to be able to do so. We share this privilege of serving persons who are developmentally disabled through training programs for teachers, child care workers and aides, through public education efforts—lectures, tours, and parent counseling—and through publications and research projects.

2 Surveying the Problem

Developmental disability is gradually replacing the term "mental retardation." A slow rate of maturation, reduced learning capacity, and inadequate social adjustment result in a condition similar to developmental disability as defined in the following paragraph. Mental retardation persists into adulthood and is characterized by faulty development of intelligence which impairs an individual's ability to learn and to adjust to the demands of society.

A definition in the Developmental Disabilities Act, 1978 extension, describes developmental disability as a severe, chronic condition due to a mental or physical impairment, or combination of both, manifested before a person reaches the age of twenty-two years, and likely to continue indefinitely. The condition combines functional limitations in three or more areas of major life activity, including self-care, receptive and expressive language, learning, mobility, self-direction, capacity for independent living, and economic self-sufficiency. The person affected needs a combination and sequence of special treatment with services individually planned and coordinated.

The concept may be in transition. So also is the trend to refer to mental retardation as developmental disability. The need for an individual approach in treatment and training remains the same. Each child, each adult must be viewed as a whole person with individual characteristics. All educational, spiritual, social and physical needs call for individual planning, coordinated for relating to other people. Every disabled adult requires individualized opportunities for training, treatment, social adjustment and, if possible, self-support with contribution to fellow human beings.

Causes and characteristics of mental retardation as found in adults have their roots in earliest childhood. Parents of newly born infants that show signs of disability are often both appalled and confused. The term "developmental disability" has little meaning for the average citizen; it is something that happens in other homes but never in one's own family. As these parents face a situation which seems to be shared by few other people, lack of access to information may cause them to feel utterly alone.

Actually, they are far from being alone. Estimates indicate that 3,900,000 persons in the United States have severe developmental disabilities. The number of those moderately or mildly handicapped is greater, and it is more difficult to gauge the total number. Approximately 4,180,000 children of school age are receiving individualized educational programs. We need to realize that these individuals can continue to grow mentally throughout life if appropriate programs and experiences are provided.

Developmental disability spares neither class, race, nor creed, but the incidence rate is somewhat higher in areas where underprivileged environment aggravates the initial cause. Statistically, predictions indicate that of every 100,000 children born in this country, some 3,000 will be mentally retarded. These children are human beings awaiting understanding and help. They can be born into any family as there is no immunity.

A small percentage of mental retardation is considered directly due to hereditary predisposition. For the majority of developmentally disabled persons this condition results from accidents of one type or another, either during pregnancy, at birth, or shortly after birth. Forms of mental defect, in the past attributed to a mysterious act of God, now through research are recognized as the result of accidental causes operating before birth or during infancy up to the age of about four years. In this way mental retardation, or developmental disability, differs from the results of brain damage suffered later in life after normal growth has taken place.

At birth a low Apgar score indicates a problem. The Apgar Scale, developed by Dr. Virginia Apgar, now deceased, is used routinely in hospital delivery rooms. At one minute after birth and again four minutes later, the test provides norms for a physician to judge quickly the health of an infant according to heart rate, respiration, muscle tone, reflexes, and color—such as an extremely pale baby or a blue baby due to lack of oxygen. Signs of intercranial pressure, such as vomiting and convulsions, are also critical.

Although a larger percentage of our total population is represented among the developmentally disabled than is subject to heart ailments, cancer, polio, and other highly publicized afflictions, knowledge and understanding of mental retardation are not yet sufficiently widespread. Parents may find that even the family doctor lacks the experience and special training in this field to give adequate advice when a baby with obvious handicaps is born into a family.

An acquaintance called me one day and said that a close friend of hers had given birth to a Down's syndrome baby. The obstetrician advised the parents to have the little one transferred immediately to the infant section of the state hospital for permanent care. The pastor recommended that they take the baby home. What did I think best? My answer was the wholehearted affirmation of a personal conviction: "Take the baby home; give him love, care, and the blessing of having a family. Seek local services for infant and early childhood stimulation. At school age further decisions can be made." By that time the child was so loved and cherished that a place in the family home was assured.

Another physician told the parents, "Take the baby home and enjoy him. He'll be dead in a year"—this at a time when the great majority of Down's syndrome babies are living on through childhood, adolescence, and well into adulthood. An encouraging sign would be increased interest of medical personnel in determining causes of, and treatment for, developmental disabilities. The extent to which mental handicap can be alleviated by treatment, training and education is a direct challenge to physicians, parents and teachers.

To grasp the scope of this problem which affects not only the children involved throughout their life span, but also their parents, siblings, and society at large, we must realize that 100,000 to 150,000 babies born each year in the United States add to the number of developmentally disabled persons. Because of improved medical and nursing care, the life expectancy of handicapped children has increased and is continuing to rise. Therefore, their care and education is a problem assuming proportions that challenge society. The retardation is so much a part of the individual that it will continue to demand long-range programs appropriate to the individual's age and ability level.

The symptoms can be modified by treatment and training, but are so inherent in the personality of the individual that there will be a difference between the developmentally disabled adult and the person free from observable impairment. This difference varies in degree. Mental growth may be helped or hindered during the earliest period of a child's life, as explained in the previous chapter.

Profoundly and severely disabled children, one in a thousand, are dependent on receiving care throughout life. The moderately retarded individuals, four in a thousand, are semi-dependent, capable of self-care and minimal skills, but seldom of attaining self-support. Approximately twenty-five in every thousand are mildly retarded, approaching the normal level of development.

Achievement may lead to a productive adulthood, but guidance is needed to supplement their limited foresight, judgment, and reasoning power. They can learn under intensive training to meet certain requirements of a self-supporting person. Many lack the capability of projecting such training into new and unfamiliar situations. The aptitude for making adjustments often marks the measure of success or failure, happiness or frustration.

There is scarcely a man or a woman in this country who is not familiar with the work done to help the blind, the polio victims, the cerebral palsied, and sufferers from rheumatic heart disease. Yet frequently we find that these same people who show liberal and wholehearted interest in helping the physically handicapped have little knowledge and slight concern about mental retardation, or developmental disability.

There are more than two hundred identified causes of developmental disability. In the next chapter I will contrast two handicapping conditions: Down's syndrome as compared with brain damage. These two groups make up a majority of the residents at St. Coletta School. In the conclusion of this chapter I will restrict myself to less frequent causes of mental retardation.

Children with familial or primary mental deficiency include many of the more stable among the developmentally disabled—those frequently referred to as mildly retarded, dull normal, borderline or slow learner. Some of the most successful adults from among former students at St. Coletta's emerged from this group. Individuals of this hereditary type are seldom very handicapped unless some secondary cause has increased the primary defectiveness.

It is well to remember that the entire hereditary deposit of each individual comes through the genes. Each person has a unique combination, different from everyone else, except for identical twins who inherit identical genetic input. Genes govern the traits that will be developed in later life under the influence of environmental factors. From the moment of conception a person's entire potential is contained in the genes, and from this moment the prenatal environment begins to affect the genes. Throughout the life of the individual there will be the combined influence of a complex heredity contained in the genes, and all the aspects of the environment. Often it is extremely difficult to pinpoint the exact cause of developmental disability in any one person because of the complex interaction between heredity and environment. This interaction is often referred to as the nature-nurture controversy.

Approximately one million genes are unevenly distributed upon the forty-six chromosomes normally found in each cell of a human being. Each gene produces an enzyme, and these enzymes regulate all chemical processes within the cell.

DNA, an easy term for deoxyribonucleic acid, forms a code that provides the pattern of inherited characteristics. Most of a person's traits are influenced by several genes. Because of this complexity of human inheritance, especially in regard to intelligence and personality, there remains much for us to learn.

In the history of mental retardation there are instances of too much emphasis on heredity. In 1877 Dugdale studied the Jukes family and found numerous examples of retardation with associated disorders. A follow-up study by Estabrook, in 1916, reviewed twelve hundred and fifty-eight descendants of the Dugdales and found one-half of them to be mentally incompetent.

Goddard's study of the Kallikak family in 1912 followed

two strains of inheritance. The one line, from a mentally deficient mother, had a preponderance of mentally handicapped and socially incompetent individuals. The other line, issuing from a normal mother, showed a consistent strain of economically and professionally successful persons. Both lines were traced back through six generations to when the father was a soldier in the American Revolutionary War, and to the period following his return home after the war. However, the methods of evaluation and validity of research at Goddard's time are now questioned. Also, Goddard failed to distinguish between cultural and genetic factors.

Often the hereditary factor is aggravated by underprivileged environment. Social deprivation and poor physical conditions frequently contribute to the retardation of these persons. Those who entered St. Coletta's at an early age were able to benefit by good nourishment and proper health care. A consistent program of special education, language development, values instruction, and work training prepared them for holding jobs of their own choice as adults. The feeling of "I can" may be more important than the IQ.

Joe and Elaine, brother and sister, entered St. Coletta's as school-age children. Both are now adults. Elaine left the school and was employed in a tea shop. Her homemade goodies made her popular and reflected the mastery she acquired in the home economics class. Elaine, a sensitive girl, severed all connections with the School as she did not want a special education label. Later she married and moved to another state. Joe remained at St. Coletta's where he is a paid employee in the large fruit and vegetable gardens. He is fond of children and of pets, surprisingly gentle under a rugged exterior, and a lover of the beauties of nature. Changes bother him, but in general he is content. "I have everything I want here at St. Coletta's. Why should I move?" When offered a trip to Rome, Italy, with others of the residents, Joe declined. "I've been to

Oconomowoc (a nearby town)," and he was satisfied with his travels at that time. A few years later he did take a trip to Europe with some friends from the neighborhood.

Twice within my experience of more than fifty years we have had five children from the same family enrolled at St. Coletta School. They were among the highest functioning level at the school, although in both cases incompetence of the parents was clearly evident. A mother who is incapable of stimulating her children adds to the retardation. The influence or lack of input on the part of the father can be equally significant. Both parents may be unaware of the need for language development, proper nutrition, correction of physical defects, keeping the child away from lead paint and other hazards. The dynamics of family life have an early influence and a lasting effect that can help or harm each child. The quality of parenthood affects the developing offspring. There can be a warm, loving family relationship even under adverse conditions. When this is true, economic help and concerned guidance in difficult situations could give the security needed for a child whose future depends upon the stability of the home.

Of course there is always the possibility that children limited by intellectual inheritance may also suffer brain damage or may be further retarded by an underprivileged home environment which restricts experiences and limits opportunities for development. The parents may be unaware of their children's need for special education, thus failing to take initiative in meeting the need.

There are some hereditary conditions of developmental disability in which the parents are of normal intelligence but transmit a mental defect to one or more of their children. These parents are carriers of recessive genes that affect certain of their offspring. Recessive genes, as opposed to dominant genes, are carried from generation to generation and affect the offspring only when paired with a similar recessive gene from the other parent. Most varieties of developmental disability attributed to specific hereditary factors are caused by recessive genes.

We have had several boys with *Wilson's Syndrome,* due to recessive inheritance, enrolled at St. Coletta School, and the condition also appears in girls. The facial appearance is one of friendliness, with a set expression and the teeth exposed in a grimacing smile. The condition is associated with cirrhosis of the liver and deposits of copper in the liver and the urine. Mental retardation varies in degree. There seems to be a reaching out for acceptance and friendship. One of these young men, Jimmie, said in an interview, "We don't want to be treated differently; we want to be treated just like normal people."

Another inherited condition, rarely appearing among males and even less often among females, is the *Prader-Willi Syndrome.* The exact mode of inheritance is not known. The main characteristic is obesity, usually developing between the second and third year of life. Short stature, weak muscles, infantile sex organs, mental retardation, and the tendency to develop diabetes are other symptoms. Parents are likely to be frustrated by the excessive eating habits. The appetite is voracious, and never satisfied. One mother brought her boy back to St. Coletta's several days early during a holiday vacation. This was not recent but I remember what she said: "He is eating us out of house and home, getting up during the night and eating everything in the refrigerator. Tying it shut doesn't help." Raiding cupboards where treats were kept at St. Coletta's was a problem with this boy, too. "The mother of one" in a letter published in the *Milwaukee Sentinel* (3/24/80) writes:

> Victims of the Prader-Willi Syndrome will eat themselves to death if allowed to do so. They don't care what

they eat, and have been known to gorge on rotten apples, sticks of butter, garbage and entire loaves of bread. They become extremely obese and literally eat themselves into an early grave because of their bizarre eating marathons.

A Prader-Willi child in a mental institution was caught in the kitchen finishing a three-gallon jar of jam.... Another was in a cooking class that made a dozen pumpkin pies for Thanksgiving. On the pretext of staying behind to help clean up, the child ate all 12 pies!

Successful treatment of two girls with Prader-Willi Syndrome at Lakemary Center, Paola, Kansas is reported in *Lakemary News,* Summer 1979. Non-stop eating was curbed through motivating Cecelia and Joy to cooperate in a carefully scheduled diet plan. Cecelia weighed 121 pounds when enrolled at the age of seven, and Joy weighed 238 pounds when fourteen years of age. Their lives were changed and positive reinforcement became personal delight as Cecelia went down to 74 pounds and Joy to 118 in two years, with 105 pounds as her goal.

Measured portions of the regular menu, with substitutes for high calorie foods, were basic to the reduction program. The improved self-image helped Cecelia and Joy to become leaders, in some instances, in their classrooms and residential groups. Cooperation of parents and family can assure continuation of the changed eating habits. Cecelia, still at Lakemary Center at this time, has retained her weight loss. Joy reached the age limit and moved to another program where she has been successful.

Mental retardation may also result when there is an inherited physiological defect, such as lack of thyroid or intolerance of protein. Most babies are born healthy but one out of sixteen may have a defect that will affect development in later life. Hereditary influences are programmed into a child's life from the earliest moment of existence. They are part of the parents' genetic characteristics and may cause changes in the egg or the sperm, or in the newly fertilized ovum. Modifications may occur in the rapidly developing embryo. The earlier any damaging effects take place, the more disastrous they will be.

Among the genetic factors causing developmental disability are the *inborn errors of metabolism.* These are an area of current medical research. One rather rare hereditary condition is *phenylketonuria,* or PKU, in which diagnosis is based on the excretion of phenylpyruvic acid in the urine. This condition responds to dietary treatment in early life. A synthetic diet, which can be phased out at the age of about eight years, provides the protein necessary for growth. Diagnosis in early infancy, followed by control of food intake, can prevent excessive brain damage.

Although mental defect is sometimes severe, physical development can be average. Leroy is a former student of St. Coletta School whose athletic build, clear blue eyes, alert expression, friendly smile, and gold-brown hair made him a handsome lad. An intelligence quotient of 50 indicated only half the aptitude normal for his age. The parents recognized Leroy's special needs but the experimentation with synthetic diet was too late to help him.

During the first few months at St. Coletta's Leroy clearly showed immature and emotionally unstable behavior. He fought for things he wanted, cried if he could not have them, refused to share with others, hesitated to attempt anything that required effort, and rebelled against the ordinary give-and-take of group companionship. Leroy had quite a difficult time developing work habits but did fairly well by the end of the year.

Improvement stemmed from the fact that Leroy's attitude toward religion was positive. He remembered and put into practice lessons learned from the example of those about him. To help a developmentally disabled individual it is strategic to begin where his chief interest lies. This motivation becomes the force through which further improvement becomes possible.

Progress in school kept pace with Leroy's growth in social maturity. He was honestly proud of learning to read and took special interest in his class activities. Most satisfying was his emotional growth. Consequently Leroy became a happier and more cooperative boy. Much of Leroy's progress resulted from an environment where undue stress was eliminated. His educational and social program was adjusted to his level of development. Leroy's progress is based on comparison with his own past record; he was helped but not cured.

Leroy returned to his family and is now an adult. His two sisters, Roberta and Marva, also have phenylketonuria. Roberta writes:

> Leroy and I are renting an apartment. Jobs are hard to get. Leroy and I share the bills. We are all working in the Glenwood Activity Center. Leroy fills mold for ceramics and I paint some ceramics. Marva sorts cans and newspapers.
>
> Leroy and I went to a party. We went out for supper at the Golden Wheel and then went dancing. I went bowling. Leroy and I went to a concert.... The harp music is just beautiful....
>
> Before we went home we had a Thanksgiving party for parents, board members, and others.... We had three turkeys. I made a green bean salad. I had to teach the others a song so I taught them, "Over the River and Through the Woods." Then Leroy and I sang, "Let There Be Peace on Earth."

This letter from Roberta gives insight into the adjustment possible on an adult level within the limitations of mental handicap. Additional comments by Roberta regarding athletic events and an art show demonstrate the value of leisure pursuits. An aesthetic appreciation of music and art enriches the person while giving enjoyment.

A newly discovered genetic defect called *"Fragile X" Syndrome* was identified recently as the second most common cause of mental retardation in the United States, according to *New Directions,* National Association of State Mental Retardation Program Directors, Inc., September 1981. Park S. Gerald, M.D., a professor of pediatrics at Harvard Medical School, says that the inherited disease occurs in one of every 2,000 to 3,000 males born. Dr. Gerald states that this occurrence is second only to Down's syndrome which happens once in every 1,000 births. He also reported that the defective material is passed from generation to generation through the females in the family, and that many cases of mental retardation attributed to it might be prevented by genetic counseling.

Prenatal diagnosis and early surgical treatment of congenital defects are based on advances of science in delicate and critical areas. Genetic counseling should not lead to abortion but rather to improving the human being during its first months of existence. Ultrasound scanning and amniocentesis, to be discussed further in our study of Down's syndrome, should never lead to a direct attempt on the life of an innocent unborn child.

Microcephalus is a rare condition of developmental disability involving a hereditary factor. There is one family history in which two children, the father and the grandfather all had the abnormally small head and birdlike profile outlined by a prominent nose with receding forehead and chin. However, there are other recognized causes aside from heredity. Radiation from X-rays of the mother before the child's birth has been identified as resulting in some instances of microcephalus. There is also danger that radioactive fall-out threatens to increase developmental disorders, such as microcephalus.

Some microcephalic babies are born without the delicate "soft spot" usually found in the skulls of normal infants. Most often retardation accompanying this condition is severe. The exceptions do well in classes planned according to their individual mental capacity. Because of the physical stigma, mainstreaming may cause tension. One mother with a thirteen-year-old microcephalic boy feared a behavior problem because the other children teased him constantly. They nicknamed him "dummy head," and attracted by his small cranium they also called him "pinhead" and "peanut head."

The children probably did not mean to be cruel but this boy was bright enough to be sensitive about his appearance. When enrolled at St. Coletta School he made an excellent adjustment. His former attitude had been that of an underdog, determined to hold his own by fighting back. To find himself accepted by classmates was a new and gratifying experience. Opportunities for leadership and for special activities in dramatics, music, and religion motivated his best efforts. Neatness and accuracy were qualities he carried into adulthood. James had the friendly, cheerful attitude found in many microcephalic persons. Like others, they are fond of attention.

I recall visiting a large state institution where there were identical twin microcephalic patients, aged about forty years. Neither of them could speak. One of the twins immediately noticed the entrance of a visitor into the crowded dayroom. She found her sister and they placed themselves, side by side, directly in front of me. The guide explained that these microcephalic twins were rather famous. They had often been photographed, and were frequently observed by visitors because of the typical configuration of their tiny heads. The peculiar "pine cone" shape, and not merely the small head size is a criterion of microcephalus.

Hydrocephalus is a condition quite the opposite from

microcephalus. The cause is usually congenital, but not hereditary. This implies that it is acquired before birth but is not transmitted in the germ plasm from the parents. In hydrocephalus the head is abnormally enlarged by an excessive accumulation of cerebrospinal fluid. Nature protects the brain by surrounding it with a watery substance that cushions any blow or shock. Oversecretion of this fluid, or an obstruction interfering with its circulation, causes pressure that forces the enlargement of the skull and inhibits the growth of the brain. If the condition is progressive, the constantly increasing pressure causes paralysis, wasting away of the body, and early death. When severe distention occurs before birth, a Caesarean operation may be necessary if the child is to be born alive. Milder hydrocephalus is recognized at birth.

John Holter of Philadelphia, the father of a hydrocephalic baby, worked heroically to devise a tiny valve to drain excessive fluid into the jugular vein when pressure causes the hydraulic action. Inserting the shunt valve, as it is called, is a technique successfully used by surgeons to control hydrocephalus. Holter's invention was too late to save his own child, but numerous other infants have developed normally because of his persistent efforts.

There are other rare types of developmental disability, and there are some individuals who do not fit into any specific classification. Sometimes we see an overlapping of symptoms. The human person is too complex for pigeonholes. In certain instances too little is known of family history, prenatal development, birth conditions, childhood accidents and early illnesses for exact causes to be determined. Diagnosis is a doctor's prerogative, but even an experienced clinician may be baffled by unusual symptoms associated with mental retardation. Research continues in the effort to determine causes and remediation.

Regardless of the cause, type or degree of mental retardation, there is general agreement among those who work with developmentally disabled persons that a loving, stimulating environment and a supportive structure are needed at all age levels. These advantages from early infancy and throughout life improve the individual's capacity to reach full potential, to function at the optimum mental level, to feel socially secure, and to prevent the early deterioration that affects maladjusted persons regardless of handicap.

Afton Harris, in a book by parents for parents entitled *We Have Been There,* says:

> Surviving being told that your adored child is mentally retarded is like surviving any natural disaster. One survives because one must and because the retarded child is going to need one's best efforts. That is not to say that the surviving is easy—it is not. Everything from that point on is colored by the knowledge that this child will never be able to lead a completely normal life. But it does get easier with time. There are always heartaches, but there are rewards too. One of the great rewards is that every tiny sign of progress becomes a shining thing of great importance. . . .

During my early years at St. Coletta's I learned that the school is not staffed to meet the needs of certain children because they are mentally ill rather than having the retardation associated with developmental disability. Mental illness is caused by a disturbance of proper functioning in the central nervous system rather than by lack of mental development. There is a difference in suffering from the *loss* of ability which had once functioned normally, rather than from *lack* of developmental ability.

Mental illness calls for psychiatric treatment before special education can be helpful. In the case of mental illness there is possibility of a cure. Mental retardation is not curable, although improvement is possible through training and education. Many parents find that a comparison between mental conditions and physical health give a clearer concept. A normal mind can become permanently deranged just as a previously healthy body can be attacked by a malignant cancer, gradually breaking down a physique which was once well and strong. So also when a normal mind over reaches its threshold of endurance and becomes sick, the person is a victim of mental illness. In much the same way a robust person can overstrain his physical resistance and suffer an attack of pneumonia which will leave him weak but from which, with proper care and treatment, he has a chance to recover.

Quite different is the condition of the person who from early infancy has lacked the blessing of good health due either to an inherently weak constitution or to injuries which prevent normal development. From the beginning of his existence a developmentally disabled child lacks the potential to reach at least average mental ability, or this potential is destroyed by injury or disease before the child has a good start in life. We cannot hope to add to the brain that which is lacking or has been destroyed, but we can help the developmentally disabled child to reach his top level of capability. If parents grasp this fact and, instead of looking for a cure, they direct their efforts toward developing latent abilities, the goal can be achieved.

3 *Contrasting Conditions*

Few occasions create more joy than the birth of a child who is wanted and waited for. Parents anticipate what the child will look like and their choice of a name. They speculate on first words and dream of a lifetime of achievements. The birth of a handicapped child dashes all those dreams. A long nightmare of searching for knowledge, for a cure, for hope begins.

The parents of one baby in 750 live births find that they have become the mother and father of an infant with Down's syndrome, formerly called mongolism. The condition is usually recognized at birth, and these children form about one-fourth of the severely and moderately retarded population. "Syndrome" indicates a group of symptoms or characteristics of so distinctive a pattern that anyone who has identified one of these individuals will easily recognize others.

The term Down's syndrome recalls the work of Dr. John Langdon-Down, a British physician. In 1866 he described the characteristics of these children who have a superficial resemblance to oriental people. This similarity gave rise to the misnomer "mongoloid." In regard to the cause of this condition, every normal human being has 23 pairs of chromosomes, a total of 46. The most common chromosomal abnormality in Down's syndrome is trisomy of Chromosome 21. An individual born with Down's syndrome has an extra number 21 chromosome, a total of 47 chromosomes, that determines

Down's syndrome. This condition is set at birth and cannot be remedied by treatment nor training.

Cynthia, a girl with Down's syndrome, was recently named winner of the first prize award in a contest sponsored by Marshall Field Company, Chicago, to honor mothers. Each contestant wrote a letter to her mother on the theme, "What I've always wanted to tell you." Cynthia's entry was chosen by Ann Landers in preference to fifteen hundred other entries submitted by eighteen-year-olds in the Chicago area. Cynthia's winning letter said:

> Mom, I've always wanted to tell you, thank you from my heart for not giving me away a few hours after I was born, when you and Dad found out I was a Down's syndrome baby. I may be a 'special' daughter but to me you are my wonderful special Mom. I will love you forever. May God bless you. Your daughter, Cindy.

Parents may find comfort in the assurance that children with Down's syndrome adjust readily in a special education program. Formerly it was predicted that these children would die at an early age. Now we commonly find them living into adulthood. Mary Louise, the oldest resident with Down's syndrome at the St. Coletta Alverno Cottages, is sixty-five years of age. She enjoys the personal care program and the stimulating opportunities offered to help these older residents to be their best selves through a long life span.

In a congenial environment and with kindly care, persons with Down's syndrome are among the happiest individuals one could hope to find anywhere. Their right to live, however, is being threatened in the earliest stages of life. Amniocentesis is a technique for determining if a pregnant mother is bearing a child with Down's syndrome or with other problematic conditions. The process involves extracting living cells and fluid from the placenta. These are tested for genetic conditions, biochemical reactions, and chromosomes. Two or three rare genetic conditions can be detected and treated in the womb.

If a genetic defect such as Down's syndrome is detected, then a moral question arises and in many instances leads to the decision for an abortion. This is a complex isue, approached differently from various points of view. The position I support stresses preservation of life. I believe, therefore, that a potentially handicapped child has the right to live.

The important point concerning amniocentesis is this: it is a procedure for gathering information. Most important, the majority of tests show absence of the suspected conditions and so provide relief from worry to anxious parents. When Down's syndrome or another developmental disability is indicated, the parents can receive counseling and supportive help for realistic acceptance of the situation. In some instances a Down's syndrome infant born alive is denied medical treatment or simple surgery which would allow the child to live. Public outcry and governmental intervention seek to halt such inhumanity.

Although a Down's syndrome child may be comparatively bright, the physical appearance causes these children and adults to stand out in a crowd. They are stigmatized by a characteristic pattern of features no matter how closely their behavior and abilities might compare with those of the average person.

Intensive infant stimulation and dynamic training programs help them to achieve, but often Down's syndrome individuals are not accepted because their facial appearance marks them as different. Now an Israeli psychologist, Reuven Feuerstein, advocates the work of two German plastic surgeons, Dr. Gottfried Lemperie and Dr. Dorin Radu, who have pioneered in corrective procedures with impressive results.

At St. Markus Hospital, Frankfurt, they have operated on

numerous Down's syndrome patients from ages three to twenty four years. Freed from the stigma that disfigured them, and consequently treated more normally, they have made strides in social development and consequent happiness.

In surgery taking about one hour and a half, more detailed for some patients than for others, with a series of no risk procedures:

> The doctors have generally reduced the size of each child's protruding tongue ... brought the ears closer to the head, raised hanging lower lips, altered the axis of the eyelids, raised cheekbones with small implants of silicone, raised the bridge of the nose and, in some cases, put implants into severely receding chins. (© New York Times Service, *The Milwaukee Journal,* 9/12/82)

Although this plastic surgery does not make the child look completely normal, results are encouraging. A look into the mirror reassures with a new feeling of happiness that uplifts the self-concept.

St. Coletta Homelights, April 1982, carries the account of Tricia McGee, a young woman with Down's syndrome who is employed in Madison, Wisconsin and lives at the Coletta-James group home. Tricia performed a self-advocacy service for developmentally disabled persons through testifying at a Wisconsin senate sub-committee considering the prohibition of abortion when a defective fetus is detected in the second trimester of pregnancy. Following is the complete text of Tricia's testimony, written by her and verbally delivered at the sub-committee hearing:

> Abortion is doing away with a fetus before birth. The fetus is a very small baby in the process of growing in the mother's uterus. Though the baby is very young, it is still

a baby. It is destroying someone who could grow up like you and me.

There are some things that can be done if a woman becomes pregnant and does not want to raise the child she is carrying. She can let him grow until he is born and then give him up to be adopted by others. She might even get to like the baby once she saw him face to face and become a good mother if she tries. But she should not kill or allow the baby to be destroyed.

The child might not be perfect; it may be deformed—crippled or mentally retarded. The baby might have Down's syndrome but that is not good enough to be done away with. That baby has a soul as well as a body. It belongs to God, and in destroying the fetus we are sinning against God.

If a child has a handicap, he should be helped instead of being killed. I am 21 years old. I was born with Down's syndrome. That means I have a disability. My parents told me about it when I was around 10 years old. There are a lot of things I can do.

I can swim.
I can read.
I can play games.
I can make friends.
I can listen to my records.
I can watch television.
I can make my own lunch.
I can go see a movie.
I can take a bus by myself to Chicago and to work.
I can count money.
I can sing like a bird.
I can brush my teeth.
I can do latch hook rugs.
I can cook dinner.
I can think.
I can pray.

I can square dance.
I can play the drums.
I know what is right.
I know what is wrong.
I can write letters.
I can scuba dive.
I can paint pictures.
I work at Madison Opportunity Center. I live at a group home with my friends.

My life is worthwhile. I am glad my mother didn't do away with me. I have a good life. I would hope pregnant women would think about that before they decide to have an abortion. I wish people would let others live instead of being selfish and doing away with the unborn because they are embarrassed, selfish, or poor. These are poor excuses but not good reasons. There is no good reason to kill. Others have been given a chance to live. I wish everyone had that same choice.

Tricia's grammar may not be perfect but her message is strong. Tricia learned about the importance of life at an early age. Her parents cared enough to discuss her disability with her, a disability which limits her power of abstract learning. Her belief in life and its intrinsic values is unimpaired.

Tricia's testimony reflects the value of early normalizing experiences. Down's syndrome children tend to be happy, friendly individuals, often with social maturity above expectation for their mental levels. They thrive on kindness and love.

Parents of a newly diagnosed Down's syndrome infant find perhaps the greatest comfort and help through the sharing of other parents who have learned to live with and love a similar child. Out of their own ordeal they have empathy for parents who are struggling to accept the reality of a child's developmental disability. They can also offer hope. We are past the days when parents were told to put a Down's syndrome child in an institution and forget its existence.

For many years there was a deep-seated impression that the Down's syndrome child could not be taught. Now it is recognized that the degree of retardation varies considerably. Increased opportunities for early intervention help to develop speech, so important for later learning experiences. These children are happy in school. Some achieve surprisingly well, thus giving a hopeful outlook for others. Patience and ingenuity on the part of the teacher, and the Down's syndrome child's fondness for imitating adults, help this different child to become less different.

At St. Coletta School, children with Down's syndrome are enrolled in classes with other children of similar mental, physical and social growth. Lively motivation, concrete learning through simple projects, and practice in thinking for self can be centered about the activity that counts here and now. The learning that satisfies present curiosity and thinking that solves a current problem are preferred to experiences that depend upon remote, postponed, or general interest for their meaning. A program with many gradual steps allows for tardy mental maturation.

Our schedule allows for spiritual as well as general development for the child. This training aims to establish moral habits that will save him from becoming a liability to society and an affliction to self. The individual with Down's syndrome does possess the capacity to love and to serve God. Planned classes help to increase and develop this capacity. As the concept of obligation toward God progresses, so too, does regard for fellow men including respect for authority, courtesy, and consideration for others. The majority can learn to do simple tasks well, are efficient in routine performance, and are usually content to be occupied as helpers. Occupational skills and job opportunities for adults with Down's syndrome await further development and opportunity.

The greatest handicap for any developmentally disabled person is the dearth of tolerance, empathy, and understanding on the part of the public. A world that places strong emphasis on mental alertness often shuns or ignores the person whose affliction is the inability to think and act as fast as most people. Society in general, and the family in particular, can be a positive support through accepting the developmentally disabled person with an understanding of his inadequacies and limitations.

After reaching individual potential in the classroom, St. Coletta School offers Down's syndrome persons a resident worker program. This protective employment is less demanding than the habilitation program preparing for outside employment. Others return home to live with the family, better able to participate because of their development within the school program. For these, daily life takes on an extra dimension through enrollment at a sheltered workshop.

One young mother whose story is told in my *Challenge of the Retarded Child* left the hospital feeling that her newborn baby was merely a vegetable—one who would never walk nor talk. Now her daughter, Virginia, is a young woman living at home after completing her program at St. Coletta School. Daily she goes to Opportunities, Inc. for employment suitable to her abilities. The Down's syndrome adult, carefully trained, is meticulous in performing routine tasks. Virginia's mother writes:

> Virginia left St. Coletta's when she was 18 years old. She had accomplished the one goal we hoped for—she learned to read. This achievement has enriched her life in many ways: she can read simple directions, follow the missalette

at Mass, and interpret her *TV Guide*. This takes up much of her time at home. She gained much in all areas of life while at St. Coletta's.

After leaving St. Coletta's Virginia was enrolled in the sheltered workshop at Opportunities, Inc., where she has remained. Here she is engaged in doing real work for outside firms and Virginia brings home a paycheck every two weeks. The sum is not large, but it is enough to keep her in spending money. She feels great about being able to go to a job every day and to contribute to her own livelihood. Virginia likes being able to endorse her own checks and to cash them at the bank. She enjoys the company of the other clients at the workshop and said one day, "I'm so glad I'm not handicapped." To her handicapped means having a lame leg or being physically deformed.

Virginia is immaculately clean about her person and tries to be aware of what is good for her to eat. She has an upbeat, cheerful disposition and it is a pleasure to take her with us when we meet in public. She surprises people with her wit and her delightful sense of humor. Virginia also has the ability to come right to the point in expressing herself. One day when she and I (her mother) had a hectic morning doing many errands down town, she said when we got home, "We did our did, didn't we?" Another time when we had a long delay at the eye doctor's office, she said, "It takes a long time to wait, doesn't it?" . . .

Virginia asks a lot of questions and wants things explained to her. Once when I explained something at length and thought I had done a good job of explaining, she said, "Will you please rephrase that?"

Virginia has several hobbies that keep her busy. She loves to knit afghans, and our friends are delighted to get them as gifts. She also hooks rugs and these make nice gifts. Virginia is full of rhythm and music makes her wiggle all over. She and four other girls from the workshop take a dancing lesson every Saturday and they thoroughly enjoy this activity.

Virginia's church means much to her and, I think, contributes to her well-being. I believe she has been an influence for good in other lives.

When Virginia was five years old, I, her mother wrote, "I wish I could say like so many others I read about that now I think the child is a blessing and that I am resigned to my cross, but I cannot truthfully say it. I resent the fact that it had to be my child who is exceptional."

Virginia has now reached the age of 34 years, and I write, "Virginia is now the joy of our lives, and without her our lives would seem empty and have less meaning."

Virginia was an only child, but Dennis was born into a family of several young children. The story of his early life is also told in *The Challenge of the Retarded Child*. The parents were generous in giving home care, and their love was reflected in the siblings' acceptance of Dennis although aware of his limitations. By the time Dennis was of school age there were six children in the family. His capacity for getting into creative types of difficulty made constant supervision imperative. For the mother, with two children younger than Dennis, his tendency to suddenly disappear on an adventure trip of his own meant constant strain. St. Coletta School offered the care that could no longer be given at home. Now, years after the return to his family, the mother writes:

> Over the past twenty years all of our children have married and had children. Dennis has twelve nieces and nephews, ranging from 15 months to 17 years, with two more on the way. They have all had a profound effect on each other—all good.

Dennis had further schooling after he returned home at the age of 16 years. The workshop, his coping with illness, his continued love and joy in his brothers and sisters, his undying love for the "Mets," his happiness with Dad retiring and problems of sharing me . . .

"We are three" in retirement now and are enjoying our new life style very much.

Dennis adds to the joy of family living and can be with his parents when all the brothers and sisters are married and living in their own homes. This companionship gives mutual comfort and joy—one of the greatest gifts of a Down's syndrome child or adult who is accepted and loved.

While the Down's syndrome child is usually recognized at birth, the child with brain damage may have normal appearance. In some instances this is not true. Developmental disabilities before birth may cause physical symptoms plainly visible in the newborn baby. Beginning on the birthday of their child, parents are faced with the fact that there is something wrong. The joyful aspect of parenthood is immediately marred. To face reality, accept the child as he is—a child—is a challenge to parents that requires growth over a period of time.

The child with brain damage may have a centralized disability that does not show exteriorly but is recognized later, such as defective speech, or lack of verbal expression. Injury to the motor center of the brain frequently results in cerebral palsy, with or without learning disability. Spastic movements or partial paralysis results from brain injury. In other instances, brain injury can cause learning problems without speech or motor involvement.

An interesting example is found in James, born a normal infant, who suffered encephalitis resulting in brain damage at an early age. During his school years he progressed slowly, displayed a love for music, liked vocational types of activity, and frequently was in trouble because of behavior problems and outbursts of anger. In December of 1957 he terminated his program at St. Coletta School and returned home.

Now, as an adult, he is known in his local area as "Iron Man," descriptive of his lean, muscular body and the arduous hours he spends in bicycle trips from Philadelphia to various parts of the country. Typical was his vacation visit to friends at St. Coletta School. Through Michigan to Wisconsin James cycled 650 miles in five days. His well-worn road maps showed careful planning which kept him on country roads rather than on busy highways.

James began his bicycle hobby by riding seventy miles each day from home to the farm where he was employed. Although suffering under the strain, James was determined to make his own way. His own way included a long series of challenging feats which resulted in his tanned, sinewy body and a fund of knowledge about the terrain he has covered. Some of the rides had a dual purpose, such as bicycling one hundred and sixteen miles—the most of any participants—in the Boca Raton, Florida Bikathon to benefit autistic children. In his journal James meticulously documents every trip, recording destination, mileage, time, weather conditions, together with observations on the people he meets and places he has seen.

Accompanying James on his training trips during the winter is his appreciation for classical music. He pedals away to the accompaniment of Bach, Handel, Mozart, Haydn, and Ravel among his favorite tapes.

The determination with which James pursues his hobby is a personal characteristic. Individuals who have suffered damage to a specific area of the brain may have other compensating abilities controlled by unimpaired areas. I am inclined to think that each of us has suffered at least minimal brain damage, not resulting in a general disability but making the level of development less perfect than indicated in the original potential. Each of us has been affected by prenatal conditions, has gone through the trauma of birth, and has been subject to early childhood illnesses, bumps and bruises. Kinship with those who have been more severely affected, empathy for the developmentally disabled, keeps us mindful of Him who would not break the bruised reed nor quench the smoldering flax.

Brain injury varies according to the area where the injury occurs and the severity and extent of the disease or accident which damages or destroys brain cells. Obviously a brain injury cannot be inherited. It can happen to any child of any parents.

Brain damage, depending upon the extent, location, and severity of the injury, may cause deafness, blindness, impediment of speech, defective intelligence, lack of coordination or loss of bodily movement, or seizures. Emotional problems often result from the difficulty in coping with the environment and the stress of interaction with other people.

The slightly deficient or mildly brain-damaged person may be the least understood of all handicapped people. The individual with minimal brain damage does not receive the consideration given to a physically crippled person. Slowness of thought and action, awkward movements and lack of precision seem exasperating when normal reactions are expected. Training in skills for self-care and preparation for job placement are time-consuming. The effort is less discouraging with the realization that this individual was spared severe brain damage causing much greater, or total, incapacitation.

Symptoms of brain damage may vary from one individual to another. Perceptual difficulties, inability to coordinate parts into a whole, distorted vision of the printed page, confusion in following directions, disorientation of time or space, and inability to follow correct judgments based on sensory experiences are some of the harassing problems disturbing the person with brain damage.

Brain-injured children in the classroom, and elsewhere, seem highly distractible because they attend to everything in the environment. Learning to concentrate on the center of interest is an important aspect of training for adulthood. Persons suffering the effects of brain injury have more than the usual difficulty in controlling their impulses. They are generally uninhibited. An essential feature of their education is to teach them over and over again to establish acceptable patterns of behavior.

Sudden loss of control due to frustration or interruption of routine can lead to an explosive reaction. Violent response to a trivial or unknown cause subsides quickly if the attention is diverted. Perseveration, a negative form of perseverance, leads to constant repetition of words or actions. The same question is repeated even if an answer has been given. Hyperactivity finds expression in meaningless actions or rhythmic body movements.

A brain-injured person finds support in basic patterns that control the activities of the day. Irregular schedules and unexpected events are upsetting; even surprises planned to give pleasure trigger the opposite reaction. Precise directions, brief commands, enunciating carefully and allowing space for comprehension are worth the time and patience required.

The person with brain damage finds security in an established routine, with the day structured in precise activities carefully sequenced over a period of time. Changes of routine are introduced gradually with preparation for the adjustment to be made.

Setting a goal and striving consistently toward it presents more than the usual difficulty for an individual who is neurologically impaired. In *We Have Been There* (© 1979, Dougan,

Isbell and Vyas Associates) a mother tells of her daughter who came home jubilant because she had made only forty-nine mistakes in her training program that day. The day before, she had made sixty-five errors. That was progress! Encouraging approval supports the effort to keep on trying. Beneath each struggle is a person with deep-seated need for friendliness and understanding.

4 *Uniqueness of Person*

In any group of people we find that no two are exactly alike. Even identical twins, whether brought up together or apart, react individually to the influences of environment, often with striking similarities but also with unique differences. This observation is also true of persons with developmental disabilities.

The person with developmental disabilities is different from other people, but who of us can feel free from all forms of handicap? While strengths of the average person far outweigh the weaknesses, still there is sure to be some area of ability less perfect than other aptitudes. Not all are gifted in music; some may have difficulty in learning languages or the abstractions of mathematics. The skills of a star athlete are not equaled by the applauding fan. Some persons are outstanding in kindness and compassion, while irrational terrorists undermine the peace of innocent people. Society recognizes many differences, and among them is mental retardation.

A child may be retarded, but first of all he is a *child,* deserving of every consideration due to the dignity of a divinely created human being. This dignity calls for respect at all levels, all ages and walks of life. This is where we must see the person, not the condition of mental retardation. We need to see the loving heart, not the slower intellect; the longing to be accepted, wanted, cared about, appreciated, instead of the rejection that doesn't give the handicapped individual a chance to be his best. We need to acknowledge a person's uniqueness, help to develop the optimum level of achievement, without manipulating conformity to unnecessary restrictions.

The developmentally disabled person has the same fundamental emotional and social needs as other people and can have a healthy personality only when these needs are satisfied. In this truth there is comfort and also challenge for parents and family members of persons with mental retardation. Like the normal person, these individuals need to feel secure in their relationships with others. They want to love and be loved. They need the satisfaction of work within their capacity, well done and appreciated as their contribution to the needs of others. Personal cleanliness, proper behavior, acceptable manners and appropriate clothing help them to feel comfortable and at ease.

When we think of people we do not necessarily ask how much intelligence they have. The more important question is, "How well do they use their intellectual gifts, limited though they may be?" When the handicapped person puts his whole self into a task and thinks he has done a good job, the results ought to be evaluated from a positive point of view. Sincere, generous praise can provide effective motivation for further effort and a greater degree of success.

There is danger in becoming so involved with the problems of the developmentally disabled persons that we look upon them as *problems*. Quoting Sister Sheila Haskett:

> We must become aware of the wonderful gifts that these handicapped individuals have to give us—the wonderful gift of recognizing the innate goodness and value of other persons, for example, the beautiful gift of a grateful heart that remembers the giver long after the gift has disappeared. We must recognize and humbly receive these gifts before we can say that we truly love this handicapped individual. The greatest gift we can give a retarded child is the opportunity for him to give to us. We must be able to say, "Thank you" before we can sincerely say, "I love you." (*St. Coletta Homelights,* January 1973)

Those who are handicapped have a tremendous need to give their gifts as well as to receive the ones we offer them. The parent, teacher or friend who takes time to listen, to truly communicate, enhances self-worth by receiving a confidence as well as by giving attention. To allow ourselves to be accessible to persons who are mentally retarded is a humbling experience. They look beyond the mask of our self-sufficiency and penetrate any fear of self-giving.

The most beautiful example of self-giving that I know is a young woman who serves as counselor for the trainees in the St. Coletta habilitation program, Sister Mary Jeanne Quinlivan. The young people gravitate toward her because she listens and cares. They see how truly she enters into their joys, their successes, their troubles, personal problems and failures. Even after they have left the program and are employed and living in apartments or at home, they keep in touch. Telephone calls to the cottage in the evening usually begin with the query, "Is Sister Mary Jeanne there?" Her cheery response, when going to the phone, is like greeting a long-lost friend. The conversation—always in private—sustains that concept. Sister has the deep spiritual life needed in order to be life-giving to dependent persons.

Sometimes it is necessary to be reminded that the slow individual is conscious of and deeply sensitive to the reactions of others. The handicapped person needs help in learning to adapt to others so that friendships can be formed. Friends are a source of strength. Living up to the expectations of a friend provides a natural reason for doing well.

The person, regardless of handicap, who is most loved and most secure in his own family is the one who can make the best adjustment away from home. Because he feels sure of his status in the family, he has less personal anxiety when facing the world of work and adjusting away from home. Confidence in a friend, or friends, will help the growth toward individual levels of emotional and social maturity.

While every child needs a loving relationship, age-appropriate expression of affection is an important learning experience. No developmentally disabled person remains a child. The cuteness of a little Down's syndrome child, for instance, becomes objectionable and is no longer cute when adulthood calls for grown-up behavior patterns. The parents, and all who help the retarded person to develop his capacities, need to look ahead. For them as for the teacher, the results of their efforts can best be measured thirty years later. One young woman who went out on a job told me that she was laughed at for being polite and dressing neatly. Her boss told her to keep up the good habits; they would lead to promotion.

An individual who has multiple handicaps will face special difficulties. Any physical defect that can be corrected early in life should be given prompt attention. The procedure may be costly, but it saves difficulty, possibly embarrassment, in later life. Leslie Lemke of Pewaukee, Wisconsin has become well known as an example of a developmentally disabled person with a special talent. Although blind and retarded, Leslie has fantastic ability as a pianist. Only the persevering, creative efforts of his foster-mother helped Leslie to develop from a helpless young child to a celebrity of television and concert stage.

The adult who, as a child, had difficulty with the traditional school subjects looks back with appreciation to the teacher who persisted in teaching him the fundamentals. Whatever level of skill he has achieved in reading for practical needs or as a leisure-time pursuit, in writing legibly when there is a need, and in using functional number sense will make him less different as an adult.

Some handicapped persons who fail in school compensate

with manual abilities. One boy who left home because of friction over his repeated failures in school achieved remarkable success as an automobile mechanic. He found among his associates the support he failed to receive from his own parents, but he had to depend upon others for all written messages except the signing of his name.

For many persons who are mentally retarded their sense of personal worth is built up by the work of their hands. However, manual skills and abilities vary in these individuals just as they do in any group. Some persons with mental retardation have inherited artistic tendencies but are limited by impaired mental functioning. My friend Billy does amazingly detailed drawings of large buildings, suspension bridges, staged events—anything that takes his fancy—but needs the protective environment of a sheltered work program. His tendency to tease by telling people how beautiful they are is accepted by some but is a source of irritation to others. Billy does find satisfaction in knowing that some of his drawings are sold as framed pictures and are also illustrating a twelve-month calendar. He wants to do these drawings for the school which has become his home and he expresses satisfaction over his contribution.

The creative ability of developmentally disabled persons is a comparatively new area for investigation. All too often potentialities are left dormant because no one has tried to develop individual urges for originality. Early efforts to create need to be encouraged. I have seen posters displayed, such as for Fire Prevention Week, which seemed crude until it was recognized that they were the best efforts of persons much younger mentally than their physical growth suggests. On the other hand, some developmentally disabled artists portray their unique perceptions of the world about them in a personally stylized manner that is outstandingly beautiful.

The story of Yoshihiko Yamamoto is told by Akira Morishima in *Psychology Today,* June 1975. Marginal lives, such as faced this Japanese lad with an IQ score never above 47, are enhanced when superior creative ability breaks through a dull exterior.

Yamamoto could not talk and was not toilet trained when old enough to enter school. He suffered from the cruel taunts of his classmates. On one occasion his misery caused him to run away. At the age of twelve years, scoring a 23 IQ and with a mental age of three years, Yamamoto was finally placed in a special education class. There the teacher, Takashi Kawasaki, liked the boy who gradually began to smile, behaved well, and slowly learned to copy letters and cartoons. Kawasaki encouraged art work through a picture diary to supply for the lack of speech. Yamamoto's class work improved as his art skills advanced. The special curriculum Kawasaki developed for the boy centered around his art work.

An accurate sketch of the Nagoya Castle, near which Yamamoto was born, had the clean lines of a print. Kawasaki had him transfer his drawing to a wood block and encouraged Yamamoto in the making of prints. This concentration led to improvement in his technique. After Yamamoto won first prize in an art contest, Kawasaki began selling the prints and using the income to provide art supplies for his student.

Although Yamamoto always had a low score, never above 47 IQ, on the Japanese version of the Stanford-Binet Intelligence Test, he did have superior visual performance as contrasted with poor verbal and abstract abilities. This pattern of one special talent is an incentive to merit teachers' attention. As they work with low functioning students there may be a hidden talent waiting to be discovered. Persistent effort and encouragement are needed to develop this unique gift. An individual who is developmentally disabled does not foresee the life and spirit that grows through artistic achievement.

Low ability for transfer of training, or lack of carryover

from one situation to another, also makes it difficult to prepare the developmentally disabled person for the responsibility of new experiences. Such qualities as initiative, foresight, judgment and will power are likely to be at a low level. Therefore, repetitive tasks are satisfying to some retarded persons; others are bored and fail to give the attention needed for accurate repetition.

Years of training may result in developmentally disabled persons becoming partially or even totally self-supporting, but seldom self-governing. They may be late in emerging from adolescence and continue to need protection and counsel. Stability and emotional maturity are essential to successful independent living. The majority of persons with mental retardation lack these qualities in varying degrees. Often they are quite deficient in self-evaluation, inclined to over-estimate ability. One young man who was successful in his job taught himself to play the accordion as a hobby. This was fine, but he entered a music competition far beyond his performance level, and was hurt by the humiliating experience. He deserved credit for trying, but did not get a positive response when he assumed a responsibility to which he was not equal.

Achieving dignity and respect for all handicapped people calls for constant struggle against prejudice, ignorance, fear of someone who is different, misunderstanding, apathy, even pity and guilt. Later we will consider some of the breakthroughs from the past that now benefit developmentally disabled persons of all ages.

Right now we are thinking of the uniqueness that makes each person an individual. While hesitating to label people, it may be helpful to clarify levels of impaired intelligence. Profoundly or severely retarded individuals usually lack verbal expression, may have gross physical abnormalities, and only minimal self-help skills. They are not overlooked in the effort to provide training. Positive reinforcement leads to gradual improvement but realistic goals are geared to small steps of growth. Even these small steps can make a great difference in their lives. An official from a state institution told me of a small group of adult patients who were barred from participation in various events because they would not wear clothing. By using treats to reinforce the length of time they retained simple garments, they gradually learned not to tear off their clothing and no longer needed to be isolated from group activities. This was a significant gain for them, but they continued to need residential care.

Moderately retarded persons show variation in the ability to express needs and preferences. They learn to perform routine tasks with pride and satisfaction. Those employed as resident workers here at St. Coletta School perform their tasks well. They are truly missed when away on vacation. Their capacity for enjoyment includes attendance at community events and local entertainment. For many of them a deep faith makes religion a meaningful influence in their lives.

There is considerable variation between persons whose IQ range is in the thirties and those moderately retarded individuals whose intelligence quotient is about fifty, around half of the normal expectation. As adults, many are able to be helpful while living at home or in a residential setting. Others are employed in sheltered workshops or opportunity centers.

Mildly retarded persons are more numerous than those on severely and moderately retarded levels. They are better able to benefit by special education and may be mainstreamed into regular classes. Functional ability is more significant for later life than the intelligence quotient. The below normal IQ indicates a certain limitation to future progress, but does not describe the area in which greatest improvement can be accomplished. An aptitude test is more likely to yield this insight.

Sensory, motor and social training in early life helps the

developmentally disabled person to reach a higher achievement level in adolescence and adult years. An organized foundation of learning skills takes its rightful place before the usual classroom work with academic fundamentals.

Although learning is initially a sensory experience, motor activity brings a child into direct contact with the environment and helps to reinforce learning. Social behavior is influenced by creating interest in other persons, by developing basic religious and moral concepts, and by improvement of speech and language. Emphasis in these activities is on understanding, formation and expression of ideas. The developmentally disabled person who has learned to read tends to be more at ease with his peers through enjoyment of books and the utility of reading signs, directions and at least the headlines of newspapers.

Work with developmentally disabled persons has to be judged by human values, and these appraisals are too often subject to error. What yardstick can measure the uplifting power of understanding and help given to those who have difficulty in helping themselves? Regardless of variation in appearance and ability, handicapped persons are particularly in need of acceptance and love. The value of these relationships is increased through the day-by-day process of living with a developmentally disabled person. There must be a constant readiness to assist in both pleasant and painful experiences. Careful attention to emotional needs helps the person to become more acceptable to live with, wherever his life will be spent. The individual who responds well to social training can become a happy influence in family or group life.

Good habits of conduct and wholesome attitudes of mind enable the handicapped person to live happily on his own mental level in accordance with the plan of the Creator. Much can be accomplished through encouraging a hopeful attitude, believing that developmentally disabled persons can be helped, and that it is a God-given privilege to work with them. The whole person is much more than an intelligence quotient can indicate.

The significant question is not whether an individual is congenitally undeveloped, brain-damaged, or a victim of poor heredity or underprivileged environment. The important issue centers on whether the child is accepted as a human individual with a personality that is unique to him, a creation of God with a right to happiness and a possessor of limited ability to function with his peers. The fruition of this ability, limited though it may be, is fundamental to the emotional needs of the developmentally disabled person.

True emotion is strong and beautiful, an essential part of human nature. Emotion cannot be eliminated, no matter how much the outward expression may be controlled or denied. Developmentally disabled persons respond more readily to emotional than to intellectual appeal. They can more easily be reached through the heart than through the head. The powerful force of human emotion, if properly guided, is capable of assuring the productive peace that God's love provides.

The child can remain emotionally secure and retain his confidence in the goodness of his parents when he knows that he is loved by them at all times, even when he makes mistakes. He needs to know that this love will not waver nor fail when his behavior needs correction. His parents may disapprove of an action while making the distinction between the offender and the offense.

Emotional problems are sure to result when the developmentally disabled person is compared unfavorably with normal people. The hurt to the self-concept wounds deeply. Although some handicapped children are not emotionally disturbed, the feeling of being different causes a problem often enough that it warrants consideration. Emotionally disturbed children display fear and rage; they are restless or listless, too upset to use the ability they have; they fidget, they fight; some are dreamers, other are bullies. The emotional disturbances found among handicapped children are of the same variety as those found in an average group.

Conflict in a home, a broken home, parental rejection, insecurity, fear, anxiety, excessive noise, over-crowding and sibling rivalry breed emotional stress. The child may be a victim of, rather than an active participant in, the problem. The handicapped child is sometimes cast in the scapegoat role, with all the family problems being attributed to him or her. When this child is removed from the home, there is a revelation for the family. Misbehavior of the other children, or even of the parents, suddenly becomes evident as they discover that the handicapped person actually served as a protective mask for them. These difficulties can involve a child who is retarded, or they can cause apparent retardation in a child who is inherently normal. Foster home placement may give such a child the climate needed for optimum development, or family counseling might be helpful.

The professional services of a child psychiatrist may be needed to remedy the injury to a child's personality and to initiate, or restore, confidence in adults. When the conflict involves the child-parent relationship, change of environment is not enough. The child will project the feelings he has toward his parents into the new situation and relate these feelings to the persons who are taking their place.

This transfer of resentment might not be openly expressed. The overly good child who does not show his emotions may be the one who is hurting most deeply. Life is hard enough for a child when he realizes that he is not able to compete with other children. If those he loves—particularly his parents—stress his failure, the hurt becomes unbearable. In this painful process he learns to hide his wounds, but when he thinks himself unnoticed, he may try to even accounts. The child might seem to be sly or mean. He is a child who needs help.

One little boy, Dan, of about 60 IQ level, is clever at remembering what types of teasing upset the boys in his group. Suddenly someone near him will scream. Dan looks perfectly innocent, but there is a triumphant gleam in his eye if the child who screamed receives a reprimand. Dan becomes more overtly aggressive as he finds that he can no longer get away with his hidden manner of causing a disturbance. When such a child makes no effort to conceal his anti-social conduct and seems to be at his worst, he may be at the point where he is ready to respond to behavior modification. Often these disturbed, insecure children are most annoying just before they begin to improve.

Persons who work with emotionally disturbed children need the experience and understanding to realize that a child's behavior is symptomatic of his feelings. Parents will find that supplying words for their child in an attempt to ascertain his pent-up emotions may give the relief he needs. Unaided he might be unable to express himself. The underlying cause, as well as the behavior problem itself, needs attention. There must be a sincere effort to free the child from his unhappy tensions before it is too late. The earnest desire to help a troublesome child is the first requisite for effective handling of difficult problems. Adult adjustment depends upon solving early signs of maladjustment. The children of America are its treasure and its hope; developmentally disabled, average, or gifted, each child merits due consideration.

Emotional immaturity in the adult may be due to lack of insight into a total situation. Mental growth has not kept pace with physical growth in the developmentally disabled person. Emotional maturity implies intellectual insight into one's own feelings as they react to persons and situations.

Inappropriate behavior often indicates emotional immaturity. Asking personal questions, disregarding the privacy of others, hugging and kissing without regard to time or place, uncontrolled outbursts of temper—these are a few manifestations of emotional immaturity. We do no favor to the handicapped person by permitting this type of behavior. Anything that draws unfavorable attention or makes the person conspicuous makes it difficult for the person to be accepted in a group. Emotional outbursts may result from frustration in meeting the demands of social adjustment. Handling frustration in a mature manner is a challenge to every person, and especially so when handicapping conditions add to the frustration. Some reflections on emotionally mature behavior may give a constructive approach toward building this maturity.

Concerned friends can model for the disabled persons appropriate responses to joy, affection, disappointment, sadness, sympathy, exultation—whatever the occasion requires. Considering mature behavior offers a guide when dealing with immature responses.

Maturity is unselfishness, responding to the needs of others. I have observed in adults who are handicapped a special kindness toward those who are more severely afflicted. At one time a large group of physically disabled persons were on pilgrimage with St. Coletta School as a destination. Their enjoyment was free of the restrictions that physical disability might have imposed. St. Coletta residents responded to individual needs—lifting when needed, pushing wheelchairs, offering a supportive arm—so that even severely handicapped guests did not miss a thing. They visited every room and saw every activity.

Maturity also calls for patience—the willingness to postpone gratification. Developmentally disabled persons may yield to immature behavior when they lack the judgment needed to pass up immediate pleasure or profit in favor of long-term satisfaction or gain.

Emotional maturity calls for the ability to handle frustration, control anger, and settle differences without violence or destruction. The emotionally mature person can disagree without being disagreeable. The gift of remaining calm in the midst of tension brings peace, not only for the individual but for those in the group or whose lives are touched by the calming influence of an emotionally mature person.

Sweating out a task, completing a project, and persevering in spite of difficulty are mature qualities enabling a person to face unpleasantness without becoming bitter. A mature person is able to say, "I am sorry," or "I was wrong," and when he is right, he does not need to say, "I told you so!"

Learning to make choices is an important part of development in the disabled person. This growth experience helps the individual to make a decision and then to accept responsibility for the outcome. Maturity means dependability, integrity, keeping one's word. Among the developmentally disabled there are persons I know who are limited but can be relied upon to come through with whatever they promise. Others are immature, make excuses, are tardy and unreliable, although possibly well meaning and even unaware of a persistent childishness. In this way, as in many others, developmentally disabled persons are like the average population.

Dignity and self-respect are enhanced by actions and life style appropriate to age. The mode of dress should not draw undue attention as this would exaggerate any inappropriate speech or behavior. Adjustment should relate to the pathway of life. A letter received from a former student at St. Coletta's gives evidence of adjustment as a farmer's wife:

> My first experience with farming was at St. Coletta's. I didn't think then that I would ever get back to it. I married a farmer—a very good one! We live about three miles from the town of Wiggins, Colorado. On our farm

we have 160 acres at the home place. We have a sprinkler that is one-fourth mile long and we flood irrigate besides. Most of the land is in corn with about five acres of hay. I have learned a lot about what it takes to get the land ready before the seed goes in. Then it is continuous work cultivating and controlling insects. We also have to worry about hail harvesting our crop before it is ready. We have 320 acres of dry land on which we grow wheat. We have to depend upon Mother Nature to provide the moisture. For the past two years we have used a combine for our corn crop. We also have corn contest plots for which trophies are awarded. This year the contest plot yielded 208.26 bushels per acre and my husband, Kenneth, will again receive a trophy. We have a garden and a dog. A friend of ours has a cattle ranch and we help him brand his calves. It is a very interesting and rewarding life. I love being a farm wife.

On a lower level of intelligence but also showing emotional growth is Joe, recently returning home after thirteen years at St. Coletta School. Joe's mother writes his story and I am quoting a few paragraphs:

> By the time Joe was seven years old he was so hyperactive that our family was in deep trouble. I had been told not to be too tough on Joe so he was quite unmanageable and wore us all out with his excessive energy. He had destroyed three sofas with his endless bouncing and I couldn't keep up with him any more. . . .

The parents applied for Joe's admission to St. Coletta School and were given the encouragement they needed.

> We came home convinced that you could help Joe and that you wanted to. Two or three weeks later, we had done the most momentous thing in our lives—given Joe to

you to care for and nurture.... Gradually we became aware that he wouldn't read and write but because of the way he has been educated that never really mattered. We have been able to rejoice in the way his personality has developed and we now feel that Joe's most important asset is his positive attitude about himself and others....

At home Joe is such a blessing to our family.... His pleasant personality is our biggest delight. We have yet to see any sign of negative thinking or actions! He is not demanding in any way and is very cooperative in all areas. Doesn't it seem almost too good to be true? We are so grateful for the training he had and we also thank God daily for making Joe the way he is ... the end "product" a whole human being with functional skills and a marvelous self-image—and a pleasant personality....

Uniqueness of person reaches a goal when the developmentally disabled person, after a structured program of training, finds a place in life that is satisfying to individual interests and needs. Appropriate placement will vary from a sheltered environment to competitive employment. The value of an individual is expressed not only in what he does, but also in who he is—a human person who affirms life.

5 *Family Attitudes*

A strong measure of happiness is found in the home where every family member finds assurance of love and understanding. This security is particularly needed by the son or daughter who is in some way exceptional. True understanding is reached when parents are able to see each child as unique, created by God to fulfill a certain purpose in life. Wholesome family attitudes are built upon this simple but profound truth.

Repeatedly I meet with situations that indicate how an entire family is affected when one member is developmentally disabled. Their first reactions are likely to be negative. Anger and frustration, pity and discouragement need to be worked through so that tension is relieved. In some instances, the responsibility for a disabled member can provide the family with a purpose in life, painful though these responsibilities may be. A widow who came to visit her seven-year-old son once confided to me, "Am I glad to have him! He is the only near relative I have!" Then she spoke of her despondency following the unexpected death of her husband. Because of the child, she needed to get a job quickly, and this brought her into relationship with understanding friends who, in turn, shared her concern for the child's special education.

Parents usually cannot accept painful facts so readily. I recall one mother who was crushed at the realization that not only her first little boy, but also her second son, would never develop normally. Confused with feelings of hopeless inadequacy, she wanted to walk far out into a nearby river and be swept away so that no one would ever see her again. Then she asked herself, "How could my husband be expected to face the future—a daily struggle with two helpless children and the memory of a suicide wife?" Later the two boys were able to enter a special education program, developmentally disabled but well adjusted in a peer group. The mother and father helped each other to build a positive attitude during the changes that came with their sons' growth in years and their moderate level of progress.

There are advantages in being able to locate a handicapped child in the perspective of an entire family group. The demands of other children prevent parents from centering too much attention on the one who is handicapped. A mother of seven suffered apprehension day and night when she realized that one child was not keeping pace with the others. Her fears were confirmed when she took him to different doctors, receiving from each a similar diagnosis. Her six healthy, normal children were a support to the father and mother as they faced the need of special care for the one who would always be dependent upon them.

Striving for a constructive attitude becomes a poignant experience when all the affection and ambitions of the parents focus on an only child who is developmentally disabled. They may tend toward over-protection, further delaying growth by shielding the child from experiences that could stimulate development. On the other hand, they might be too demanding, determined to force normal development from a child who does not have the ability to meet average expectations.

Sometimes parents remain unaware of slow mental growth in an only child because they are unable to match his progress with that of normal brothers and sisters. One mother said, "Having no other children we did not realize how far our little Ellen was falling behind. Neighborhood children did seem more alert, but Ellen never left my side long enough for me to know that she would be a misfit in their games. Sometimes I felt uneasy about her, and my husband worried, too. We were so sure, though, that this couldn't happen to us."

Not only the child who is developmentally disabled, but also the parents need to be understood. These parents face a long period of agonizing bewilderment over the reasons for so unexpected a problem. Probably most parents of handicapped children go through a cycle of harrowing fears, pondering whether or not the child's condition might be their own fault and seeking possible causes to absolve them from feelings of guilt.

Parents experience relief when there is someone to listen to them, to understand their feeling of possible guilt, to anticipate their need to do constructive planning for the son or daughter who is the center of their anxiety. Siblings, also, need to come to the realization of familial responsibility in facing painful facts. On the other hand, families should not despair. With increased medical interest, preventive therapy and early intervention, the painful acknowledgement of facts can become the prelude to a brighter future.

Some parents may feel the need to go from doctor to doctor, looking for reassurance or for the possibility of a cure. In this way, time and money are sacrificed. However, certain people require this means for working through their bruised feelings. Such activity forms an outlet for the frustration that builds up while facing a difficult situation.

Lack of confidence in any doctor prompts some parents to go from one specialist to another in an effort to chance upon the miraculous. They spend more money on fees than they can afford, and travel from clinic to clinic, exhausting themselves and their child. Others try to find a physician who will assure them that their child has no problem while they know in their hearts that his development is below expectation.

It may happen that the insecurity of the parents is reflected in acting-out behavior on the part of the child. Coping with these behaviors presents a new problem. Angry feelings at being different and the pressures of trying to meet expectations can cause behavior problems not only in the child but also in the adolescent or adult person who is developmentally disabled. Like other people, retarded persons are not happy all the time. To find themselves regarded as children—boys instead of men and girls instead of women—irritates the individual who is struggling with self-concept. Parents may find it difficult to recognize that the dependent child has grown to adult years and that his/her adult behavior should be fostered.

Parents should deal with anger, to confront their own and their child's! Angry feelings might be submerged but they don't just go away. They stem from defense reactions against failure, teasing, neglect, friendless isolation, anxiety, restriction, routine boredom and lack of freedom. Developmentally disabled persons have a right to be angry when they are belittled, or there is other just cause. They need help in learning to handle anger in an appropriate way. Offering outlets for energy, with reasonable goals, dispels the frustration that builds up angry feelings leading to temper tantrums in the child or outbursts of rage in the older individual.

Anger is not bad. Feelings of anger are normal and natural when there is cause. Trying to minimize the situation makes anger worse. Feeling angry is normal where there is meanness or injustice. In dealing with the anger, it is advisable to keep cool and speak softly. Reflect on what is said, and encourage the angry person to speak out about his grievance. Waiting for a better moment is sometimes preferable. After the anger subsides, review the situation. Discuss with the developmentally disabled person why he/she gets angry, and accept the anger without instilling feelings of guilt. The goal is to teach appropriate behavior when angry, not to punish for being angry.

In responding to anger, violent or destructive behavior is unacceptable. Each angry outburst should become a learning experience through involving the person in a discussion of what happened and what could constitute an appropriate response.

Discipline means teaching, and respect is an important element in discipline. Respect can be shown by listening, giving support and encouraging acceptable solutions to provoking situations. To build a better self-concept, parents and family members must listen with sensitivity. A sense of personal worth is the best antidote for acting-out behavior. A distinction between angry feelings and angry acts forms a guideline that may require patience and repetition.

Angry people do not want advice but they do want others to understand how they feel. Encourage the hurt person to talk out until all the pain has surfaced. Then healing words can help to build the self-concept and a sense of personal worth. Listening with sensitivity provides a first step toward handling angry feelings and a first step away from angry acts that might be injurious to self or others.

Humor helps to relieve tension, but it can backfire if the person mistakes humor for ridicule. Working off anger, whether hidden or overt, releases tension through activity. It is well to remember, too, that when anger resides in over-quiet, withdrawn behavior this may be more harmful than outbursts of anger. Offering other appropriate alternatives and showing appreciation of good conduct may help the person more than anything else.

Too often the handicapped person is stigmatized for his negative qualities and his positive points are overlooked. Thus the handicapped individual becomes hurt and confused. As a consequence, the pain of the parents, brothers and sisters is more subtle because they have a keener awareness that the greater problem is their lack of understanding of the need to accentuate the positive.

The presence of a developmentally disabled member affects the family's life in every area: emotional, social, spiritual, and economic. The degree of stress will depend upon such circumstances of the home and neighborhood as give evidence of acceptance or rejection of the handicapped individual. Emotionally there is the grief of realizing that the awaited and longed for child will never develop normally. Improvement takes place through appropriate treatment and training but these do not produce a cure.

Socially the family faces the question of acceptance among friends and relatives. Some parents deny themselves all social contacts because the child requires their time or because they choose to shield him from unfavorable attention. Brothers and sisters might be reluctant to bring friends into the home for fear of embarrassment. Others will courageously challenge their friends to accept the handicapped individual. Acceptance is made easier when there is a positive attitude and when proper cultivation of social behavior helps the handicapped individual to be his best "acceptable" self.

Spiritually much depends upon the degree of confidence in God with which family members interpret the presence of a child who is developmentally disabled. The realization that God permits each joy and sorrow, and that He is all-powerful to bring some greater good out of each event, requires deep faith. There is no plan that a family makes for its well-being and final happiness that can equal confidence in the providence of God. Many people are not ready to recognize God's providence when it comes in the form of disappointment. Parents can gain from religion unusual strength to accept the sorrow they experience upon learning that their child is handicapped. I have listened time and again to parents recounting their struggle to face and accept the painful fact. Those who have found active peace are the ones who can say, "My faith in God helped me. Trust in His goodness made it possible for me to carry on."

Economically, too, a family experiences the consequences of providing for a son or daughter who has special needs. Often it is difficult to balance the normal family requirements against the expense of extra care and special education for a handicapped child. It is perfectly normal for parents to know fear and anxiety regarding the future and over their inability to find a decisive solution to their problems.

Mistakes are natural, and aftersight is always wiser than foresight. In later years some parents regret their failure to plan differently. Even if they could have done so, they might not have been ready to take a certain step when the child was younger. Time was needed for working through their personal problem. Rather than entertain past regrets, it is more realistic to concentrate on, "What can be done now that will be best for the future of our son or daughter?"

Optimum development of the developmentally disabled person in an atmosphere of acceptance, understanding, and happiness is the goal to keep in mind. A friendly, secure, well-trained person, even if handicapped, is prepared for life's daily opportunities for helpfulness toward self and others in accordance with his ability. The whole family will feel repaid for a positive attitude which enables the handicapped member to achieve his full potential.

The brothers and sisters of a developmentally disabled person are closely involved in creating a positive family attitude. Very often they take their cue from the parents. Like the parents, the siblings grow through a period of seeking knowledge about mental retardation and struggling toward acceptance of a handicapped family member. Many of these young people find it less traumatic than we are apt to expect.

Family Attitudes

Step by step, parents and all the family members—normal and handicapped—need to learn, through daily living, to live with each other. Decisions regarding a handicapped member should include this member in the decision-making process. Regard for the common good takes in the best interests of each member of the family. In the book *We Have Been There,* one mother writes:

> We try to divide our time equally between our two children, and if our non-handicapped daughter complains that her retarded brother never has to do this or that, she gets assigned to teach him to master that task.
>
> We chose to live in a neighborhood where both children could have lots of neighborhood playmates. This way, our daughter could have the freedom of going off and playing with her friends without taking her retarded brother along. But he is willingly included many times because he's the only boy who still likes to play "house." When they play school, he's the one they all like to take turns teaching.
>
> Our daughter has become very sensitive to other people's feelings as a result of having a retarded brother. When we were new in this neighborhood and other children were not as accepting of her brother as they are now, she would defend him loyally. As the neighborhood children have become more familiar with our retarded son, the unkind behavior has nearly ceased. They know what to expect now. Our family has tried to project an accepting attitude and it has been contagious. He's always included in the activities for children just as our daughter is.

At times siblings might be embarrassed, not so much because of the handicapped brother or sister, but because of the unfeeling attitude of others. Those who call names, ridicule, harass, and insult the developmentally disabled individual also hurt family members. In sharing this pain, siblings may learn patience and compassion, but they are also likely to get angry. Sometimes anger will be directed toward the handicapped sibling. Annoyances may be caused by unusual behavior patterns, destructive tendencies, or invasion of privacy.

The extra attention some parents are inclined to give a handicapped child can cause normal brothers and sisters to feel neglected. Resentment builds when undue amounts of the family income are channeled into extra services for a handicapped member, thus curtailing essentials for the family as a whole. Guilt over feelings of resentment needs to find expression and healing. Sharing in a family forum is a means of clarifying issues, giving comfort and support.

Positive attitudes during childhood are favorable to the maturing person who is developmentally disabled. The retarded sibling should be a part of, rather than apart from, family occasions such as the wedding of a brother or sister. Loyal sibling relations ease the situations from the time dating begins. Again, knowledge of the couple regarding mental retardation is helpful. Fear of hereditary factors should be cleared, if necessary, through genetic counseling.

Sister Shirley Kucera, O.S.B., in a research project conducted to fulfill partial requirements for a Master of Arts in Education degree at Cardinal Stritch College, presents this summary statement:

> In the midst of many findings, statements and implications, one fact predominates above all others in this study: that persons who are developmentally disabled are persons first and that their brothers and sisters who are normal have a right to understand the disability, to share their attitudes (positive and negative), and to be heard and accepted in the face of these feelings.

The attitudes of siblings, with those of parents and grandparents, form a pattern from which the person who is handicapped develops a concept of worth. Inclusion of grandparents can add an important dimension to building the self-worth of a person who is developmentally disabled. Concerned grandparents find that their lives are also touched, often in an intimate way, as a loved grandchild faces the adjustment of growing up while the struggle with mental handicap threatens the developing self-concept. Seeing one's self as an individual of worth becomes meaningful in sharing with others, disabled and nondisabled, in the reach toward maturity.

6　*Reaching Toward Maturity*

There is no set formula for teaching a developmentally disabled person, or any person, how to arrive at maturity. This goal means more than chronological growth and it can be accomplished only in an environment of freedom. I believe, however, that the process begins in the earliest days of life.

More and more I am convinced that the best help a handicapped child can receive early in life is home care from a loving family. God's plan for every child is that it be born into a family where emotional needs are fulfilled. Each retarded, average, or precocious infant requires the inimitable touch of mother love and paternal affection and care.

The parents of a child who shows developmental disability will find in many instances that it is possible to keep their little one at home, especially when day classes are available at school age. However, simply to keep a child at home without educational opportunities according to that child's ability is unfair to him or her. After individual circumstances are considered, parents should decide according to the needs of the handicapped child and the total welfare of the family. Individuals quite advanced in years who have been kept at home with no opportunity for training or special education face a dilemma in later life.

A letter recently received tells of a woman, mentally retarded, aged forty-three years, whose father had been killed in an automobile accident. A brother married, moved away and had quite a large family. One sister died, and then the mother, so finally the woman we shall call Jeanine was left alone with her only remaining sister who had reached retirement age.

Jeanine had no formal schooling but had good home training. The lack of education limited her greatly in choices of leisure time activities beyond watching soap operas on television. The training received at home assured that she was personally clean, careful of clothing, well-mannered, and helpful with household tasks as she was only moderately retarded. An unfortunate reaction occurred when her sister, with the intention of encouraging her to socialize, enrolled Jeanine in a local program for adults. They were more severely handicapped, and being grouped with them seemed to take away her self-esteem. Jeanine no longer cared to be helpful, became withdrawn, unhappy, now sits and rocks from after breakfast until early afternoon, and then goes to rest in her bedroom upstairs.

These indications of deterioration leave Jeanine's sister facing the problem of what will happen to Jeanine if her sister's health fails. She wants to keep Jeanine with her as long as possible, but seeks an alternative.

Jeanine's story points up the need of definite preparation for adulthood, and this includes early opportunities for individualized education. The basic steps begin at home. Greater emotional stability can be expected in later life when the developmentally disabled individual has received home care during the earliest years. After the age of six placement in a special school may be advisable, but this does not mean that the family is giving up the child, or "putting it away." The child still belongs to the family. Visits and vacations help to keep the family ties strong.

There are few perfect solutions to perplexities of life, but doctors and educators are assisting parents to plan realistically depending upon the development the child is likely to achieve. A complete study reveals the level on which the individual can be expected to function in later life. Sometimes it may seem that there is no end to tests and examinations. A comprehensive study by a team of professionally trained personnel will give the parents a better understanding of the problem presented by their son or daughter. The teamwork plan recognizes that the child can best be helped through favorable family relationships. These are achieved by fostering insight into the mutual needs of the parents, siblings, and a developmentally disabled family member.

Where there is a handicapped child in the family it is certain that devoted parents have suffered emotional stress. The child in turn has felt the repercussion of tension caused by the parents' anxiety. Thus a vicious cycle of strain is established. Many years may pass before parents can look back and see a positive side to times marked by distress. Often the parents and the normal brothers and sisters reach an unselfish maturity which they would not have attained without the so-called burden of an afflicted individual who claimed their loving attention. Sometimes a blessing comes through the friends and contacts which have resulted from the special needs of a developmentally disabled child.

This child has a certain right to the self-sacrificing care of the family if his needs can be met at home. As he grows and matures, slowly though it may be, he also has a responsibility to his home and his family. Habits of kindness, punctuality, honesty, truthfulness, faithfulness to simple duties and cheerful accomplishment of assigned tasks may compensate for lack of higher mental ability. These traits can be taught most effectively by good example. This positive training is emphasized by consistency. That which is insisted upon today must be upheld tomorrow. Consistent correction must follow each choice of improper behavior. Kind firmness on the part of parent and teacher is indispensable.

The satisfaction of pleasing others in some small way is for the handicapped child a guarantee of his own happiness. It is not so much what we do *for* these children which appeals to them, but that they *share* in the doing. The parent may gain satisfaction in acting for the child but the latter loses the experience of joy in achievement. True especially of handicapped children is the fact that they learn to do by doing. When given the chance, they frequently succeed where according to theoretical standards success could not be expected.

However, the developmentally disabled child cannot be coerced. He will set his own pace for learning. Interest is his key to achievement. A certain little boy with Down's syndrome amazed me with his progress. His mother said, "We let whatever there is in Wayne come forth of its own accord and in its own time." He is an original do-it-yourself boy and will not tolerate help when there is any hope that he can accomplish what he has set out to do. The parents have tried to foster this attitude, although it takes great patience when Wayne decides to set the table—china, silver, glassware and all. Seldom is anything broken, however. At the age of seven he showed fine manual control and a surprising sense of correct procedure.

Meeting the child at his own level is an important challenge. If the parents expect less than the child is able to do, there will be no learning. The parents who expect too much will be disappointed. Usually the child reflects the parents' feelings. A positive, hopeful attitude in working with a slow child encourages good results. A wise choice of appropriate tasks will pave the way for success. The attempt to force a child before he is mentally conditioned may lead to stubbornness. Permit him to do as much as possible by himself but be ready to give the added touch when it is really needed. Parents will find that they can help their child most effectively by praying, working, and recreating with him, at all times setting an example which will make the child want to be like other people, the people whom he is learning to love and admire.

Thoughtful adults will show respect for a child in their manner of speaking to him. The child usually responds in the manner with which he is approached. A friendly request receives better cooperation than an exacting command. Expressing honest interest and appreciation helps the developmentally disabled individual to feel worthwhile. Parents who appreciate their child's improvement will by this very fact encourage further progress. Often self-respect is at a low ebb in the handicapped person. He needs approval to support his sense of personal worth.

When compared to the average child, there will always be more experience of failure for those who are mentally at a disadvantage. Many avenues of life are closed to individuals who cannot function at a normal level. This is all the greater reason why they need to capitalize on the abilities they do have. Often these aptitudes lie in the direction of service to others. Deeds of kindness and helpfulness, performed with joy, can enrich the lives of developmentally disabled persons. Early home training is important for setting this pattern. An attitude of helpfulness should be encouraged by expression of approval since handicapped individuals share in the natural human desire for recognition.

Integration with normal peers offers distinct values for the person who is developmentally disabled. Life will be lived, preferably, among average people in normal situations. We do not like to think of segregating a handicapped person. This person is probably much more normal than different.

When it is advisable to segregate an individual from the normal peers, group living has advantages in providing companionship. The support of a group appeals to the otherwise lonely individual and gives a sense of belonging.

With the young child, parents may fear retardation if placed in a group of handicapped children. They fail to recognize that this placement will permit the child to become a leader instead of a follower, to be accepted among peers. Each person, child or adult, must learn to live in harmony with his equals in age and development. All through life he will need the companionship of his peers. Learning to live, work, and recreate with others is important for the handicapped person. He must know and respect their rights as well as his own.

For the school-age child opportunities for this learning are offered in the group situation found in a residential school. The wholesome give-and-take of group living has a strong, lasting character. This experience provides a degree of stability which can contribute much toward developing the security and potential of individuals within the residential group. There is special value in the carry-over into adulthood. Sometimes it is surprising to see self-confidence grow in handicapped persons when they find for the first time that they can compete successfully with the members of a group.

This favorable aspect is not invariably true. Pressures and tensions of group living in a residential setting seriously disturb some individuals. Maladjusted persons are likely to rebel against group restrictions or relations within the group, or with attendants. Planned routines which give security to some people can be devastating for others. The protection of supervisory personnel may bring about open rebellion in some individuals. Among children this defiance may take the form of disobedience, insolence, temper tantrums, destructiveness, truancy, or general disturbance in the group. Adults with developmental disabilities may feel resentment deeply but be less open in displaying their feelings because of behavior modification in their earlier training.

From the viewpoint of mental health the tendency toward introversion presents a more serious form of behavior than uncontrolled disturbance. Children who do not get the understanding they desperately crave may seek escape by withdrawing from reality, thus forming a pattern of self-defense that leads to regression. Thoughtful attention must be directed to the individual who is overly quiet, reserved, and unlikely to cause disturbance.

Many behavior problems are adjusted through group control. In stressing the importance of individualized treatment we must not overlook that which is, perhaps, of greater consequence—the power of the group in teaching its members to live together constructively. The pattern of conduct which has been established in a well-organized group helps to give security to a newcomer. He can readily discover what is expected of him. This fact has special value when parents have been unsuccessful in securing respect and cooperation in the earlier training of a developmentally disabled individual.

Teenage boys and girls are usually most responsive when dealt with on their own age level. This group can rise to the challenge of measuring up to adolescent deportment standards. Stimulating interest in work, play, and productive hobbies helps to channel behavior toward the forming of good habits. This is especially true on the higher levels of developmental disability with individuals who are the most capable of mischief. Alert supervision prevents unwholesome behavior from becoming habitual.

The home is the basic unit of society and the right place to lay the foundations for later adjustment to society. The handicapped person who learns to respect the property of others has acquired a valuable asset for his acceptance by the community. This learning is important in the home as well as in a residential setting or in a public area. The sense of personal worth is enhanced when each individual has his own personal things and place for keeping them safe. Even a young child who is developmentally disabled can practice the maxim, "I may touch only those things that belong to me," preventing him from stealing and damaging personal or public property.

Simple, naive individuals may offend by being too friendly; others show the opposite tendency and become offensive as a means of attracting attention. In meeting adult needs we must begin with the person, and realize that under the blanket term of developmentally disabled there are many differences. A person may be mentally handicapped, physically handicapped, or multiply handicapped. Special education, physical therapy, or a combination of both may be needed in varying degrees. An individual can be retarded mentally and also blind, deaf, or partially paralyzed and still be able to function if given appropriate training and opportunity.

All physical defects that can be corrected should have this attention early in the life of the individual. When observing at a school in Denmark I was impressed to see how many devices had been contrived to help compensate for physical disabilities. These were highly individualized, probably no two exactly the same. Teenage volunteers who worked with the handicapped students recognized individual problems and came up with accommodations that made better functioning possible. In fact, compensation for physical handicaps was at a high level.

At the core of this program was a caring attitude. Similar concern is shown in provisions that make it possible for handicapped persons to use facilities formerly restricted because of stairs instead of ramps, toilet stalls too cramped for a wheelchair patient, and curbs on street corners that presented a hazard. The Federal Architectural and Transportation Compliance Board issued in August, 1982, revised "Minimum Guidelines and Requirements for Accessible Design," specifying basic standards for making federally funded buildings reasonably accessible to developmentally disabled persons who have physical handicaps. Persons with cardiac or pulmonary problems need the consideration that permits them to function at their own pace. I knew of a young man with Down's syndrome and a weak heart who was placed in an institution. He tried to keep up, went on a hike with the residents, and the first message his family received after his entrance was that he had collapsed with heart failure.

Human Development News (November–December, 1982) describes a safety program for wheelchair patients which protects them from the fear of attack. Greater freedom is assured through this self-protection program for handicapped persons. One of the two veteran police officers who developed the program is himself a paraplegic due to an accident which occurred while on duty. For persons who are handicapped, acquiring a feeling of security enhances the striving toward greater maturity.

7 Considering Sexuality

Sexuality is a God-given gift that, rightly used, adds richness and beauty to life. Persons who are developmentally disabled share in the universal need for human intimacy, friendships and love. We see among the handicapped children with whom we work an early attraction to the opposite sex. They probably learn from older brothers and sisters the excitement of having girl friends and boy friends, a special relationship with an individual usually in the same age range.

One of the principal concerns for parents as their child matures involves sexual growth and the imparting of knowledge related to this kind of development. Early preparation is essential. When the child or young person knows enough to ask a question, an honest answer must be given. A child-parent relationship that leads to questions safeguards against unwholesome sources of sex information.

Foresight is needed in working with young children, such as those with Down's syndrome who frequently are overly demonstrative in their expressions of affection. Spontaneous embracing which is charming in a toddler needs to be controlled as the individual grows older.

Guidance is needed even in innocent expression of affection. I recall seeing two of our students, male and female in late adolescence, standing with their arms around each other, hugging and kissing in a public entertainment area. I went up to them and quietly said, "I wouldn't do that here if I were you. People might think you're retarded." This brief admonition was all the reminder they needed that certain behavior is not appropriate in public places.

Sex roles assigned by society are subtle. Actions in themselves innocent may be inappropriate in their consequences. For example, a girl sitting next to a boy strokes his thigh or pats his knee. She has no idea that he will become sexually aroused but he does. Then she is overwhelmed with fondling that she resents, but accepts, and feels guilty because she is not ready for this amorous response. She learns the consequences to a girl or woman of uninhibited behavior with a man.

Human sexuality includes more than the procreation of children. All dimensions of a person—spiritual, moral, psychological, social, physical—must be a part of sex education. The developmentally disabled teenager, like others, is bombarded by sex as portrayed through the media. People today are subjected to eroticism promoted by advertisers, movies, and television. In trying to be liberated from moral restraints, they are becoming more and more enslaved to sex. Much of what they see and hear does not reflect Christian values.

Christian moral principles are the same for the person who is developmentally disabled as they are for their normal peers. Discrimination is needed about the timing and the amount of detailed information to be given appropriately to an individual who is mentally handicapped. When parents hesitate about their ability to present sex information they may find the help they need in *The New Concordia Sex Education Series*.

This comprehensive series presents a complete sex education program adapted to the age range from early childhood through adulthood. Based on a Christian perspective, the material can be readily applied to the varying perceptive levels of children, adolescents and adults who are developmentally disabled. A multiple sensory approach is presented on six levels with textbook, study guide, filmstrip and cassette for each level. Well illustrated and clearly explained, the series anticipates even more than the usual questions. Psycho-social in its approach, the series begins with the biological and progresses through developmental stages to biblical-moral mandates. Clearly outlined, explicit, ordered and structured, the series avoids ambiguity which confuses persons who are developmentally disabled.

The handicapped person's need for intimacy is part of total development. Sensitivity to needs that are inherent ought to be part of the normalization approach. Teaching self-control can be linked with freedom in making choices between appropriate and inappropriate behavior. Self-control in all aspects of conduct aids control of sexual urges. Consistency in treating the developmentally disabled person with respect builds self-respect so necessary to preserving the dignity of a person.

Knowledge of the human body and its reproductive system should be imparted with reverence for God-given functions. Ideally, the parents should be the first to offer this instruction to their own son or daughter. Appropriate sex education, according to age and mental development, will help the person who is handicapped to enjoy rights that have often been denied. A right also presupposes a responsibility, an obligation to choose conduct according to moral principles. This moral consciousness implies clarity of instruction and freedom for the power of choice—a potential for growth. No person remains perpetually a child, cloaked in innocence based on ignorance and denial of human rights regarding sexuality.

While persons who are developmentally disabled share the genital-activity potential of other persons, sexuality is much more than that specific aspect of the God-given qualities that help a person to be lovable and loving. Each individual needs to develop those gifts of personhood that foster loving relationships with others. This sharing of life enriches the one who gives as well as the one who receives.

Young people preparing for semi-independent or independent living usually learn self-help, housekeeping and job skills, and these are important. At the same time their concerns about adult living may be centered on intimacy, sexual expression, dating, and marriage. Awareness of dangers to which their moral life will be exposed needs the support of knowing that there is something sacred, deeply personal and private about sexual experience. God's law governs the use of His gift. Religion forms the moral framework to strengthen a sense of responsibility toward self and others.

All the qualities—feminine in a woman and masculine in a man—that make up the total person are part of that person's sexual being. These values are treated in detail by a National Committee for Human Sexuality in guidelines published under the title, *Education in Human Sexuality for Christians*. The principles outlined for a Christian description of human sexuality are:

1) Each person is created unique in the image of God;

2) Despite original sin, all human life in its physical, psychological and spiritual dimension is fundamentally good;

3) Each person is created to be loved and to love, as Christ, loved by the Father, loves us;

4) Human relationships are expressed in a way that is enfleshed and sexed;

5) Human sexuality carries the responsibility to work toward Christian sexual maturity;

6) Mature Christian sexuality, in whatever state of life, demands a life-enriching commitment to other persons and the community;

7) Conjugal sexuality is an expression of the faithful, life-enriching love of husband and wife and is ordained toward the loving procreation of new life.

Some individuals need protection. I questioned why a certain young man, normal appearing and moderately capable, needed enrollment in a sheltered work situation. His mother vehemently explained: "Because he is so affectionate! He loves little children. He wants to pet and play with those he sees along the street. In our section of the city, people would not tolerate this display of affection. They'd have him arrested. When he is at home Gerald is lonesome for companionship and does not find it at his age level. We can't watch him all the time and he likes little children too well." Morally Gerald would not be doing anything wrong; socially his behavior would bring him to grief. Within a sheltered environment he has positive outlets for his natural tendencies.

In the depths of our beings as persons, we sense the imperative worth of sexual purity. Like truth, justice, love, and respect for human life, purity of life is a quality to be cherished. Handicapped persons need to know that they are free to choose sexual integrity. These persons need not be used, neither for their own gratification nor for that of another person. Sexual purity has intrinsic value. Aside from all the disintegrating factors associated with lewd living, integrity of person for the developmentally disabled, as for all other persons, calls for the chaste life designated by the wisdom and will of God.

The adolescent or young adult who is motivated to preserve self for the person who may eventually become a marriage partner is living in harmony with God's plan for the human family. Those who fail to safeguard the privacy of their sexual being may trust in God's forgiveness but have less of the integrity that makes sexual expression a joyous experience.

The right to live their own lives, to face their own responsibilities, is inherent in men and women who are developmentally disabled as it is in all persons. Psychologically, a caring attitude sustains the person who feels he is lacking an essential part of his being because he is handicapped. The feeling causes hurt and frustration in the developmentally disabled adult who faces such problems as the growing desire for dating, marriage, and having children. These are rights of every person but they are also serious responsibilities. When conducting tours, particularly of young people visiting St. Coletta School, questions often are asked in regard to dating between the young men and women in the educational and the habilitation programs. My simple answer has often been that I would discourage a young man from dating until he has a job and is able to support a wife, or the young woman until she is able to care for a household and the children she might have.

In view of their human dignity, persons with developmental disability should have the right, privilege and responsibility, insofar as possible, to make their own moral decisions. They need support and encouragement to participate in decision making to the extent of their knowledge of sexual facts and comprehension regarding the effects of sexual activity. The basic moral criterion should be the same as for all other persons: not the immediate pleasure or satisfaction, but the ultimate good of the individual in relation to the good of others.

Some things that are offensive, such as masturbation, I see as a moral problem but recognize that an individual with mental retardation may not be culpable because immoral behavior is not intended. What does masturbation say about the person's whole life right now? Is he repressed, bored, rejected? What opportunities are there for wholesome relations with others? Loneliness is a part of life, a vacuum to be filled. Giving busy work isn't enough. The individual must have meaningful activity, caring persons, the comfort of being loved.

While there are differences of opinion in regard to the moral aspects, there is general agreement that masturbating should not be done in public. Individuals who are handicapped need to be carefully taught that indecent touching is something that nice people do not approve. They also must be helped to understand that doing something secretly does not make it right. Privacy of person for bodily functions, such as toileting, should be limited to the necessary time for cleanliness. A clean body and properly fitted clothing are vital aids in preventing or controlling a habit of masturbation.

Encouraging participation in sports and in hobbies that involve physical activity helps to prevent self-stimulation that might occur when one has nothing else to do. Individuals who feel lonely and bored readily seek satisfaction through sexual feelings. Experimenting with pleasurable sensations might be a form of bodily exploration. This phase will pass as the individual matures.

In the family of an individual with mental retardation, his/her masturbation might become an embarrassment because the individual may be less self-conscious about behavior than is usual with the normal person. When masturbation is observed, it is important for the parent or other adult to keep calm. One should not focus attention on the act nor tell frightening stories of the effects of masturbation that would cause feelings of undue guilt and confusion. Medical authorities agree that there are no harmful physical effects, but masturbating can develop a form of self-love that keeps the individual from desirable social relationships. Giving the child plenty of love, with touches and caresses in a wholesome way, will help to stop the individual from forming objectionable habits.

An experienced counselor for young people who are developmentally disabled reports:

> If parents "catch" their son/daughter masturbating, I think it is important for them not to act shocked or their child will think certain feelings can't be discussed with mom and dad. People have different views on this act, even "church" people.... Some of our residents have gone to psychologists who advise masturbation as a legitimate release as long as it is done privately.... I don't encourage it. I do speak of channeling energy into other things as jogging, sit-ups.... We do talk about proper conduct in public and the respect we need to have for our own body and the bodies of others.
>
> When individuals have gotten into exploring or playing with each other's bodies, instead of giving a homily I first try to acknowledge their feelings: "I'll bet it felt good to do that." They are usually shocked that I could understand. Then I try to help them see that for people to use each other as toys or playthings, when no real love is there and no life-long commitment either, this is not respect and therefore they will be hurt by it.

If masturbation or other objectionable sexual activity persists, or becomes compulsive, it may indicate a personal, psychological, or spiritual problem. Parents who listen and encourage openness can learn the source of the problem and then help the boy or girl who is developmentally disabled to find a better outlet for pain or confusion. Feelings of shame or guilt need to be expressed. Assurance that the person is loved and the good news of God's forgiveness will reward the openness of talking about it.

Parents should prepare their child early enough to anticipate the physical changes that will take place when reaching puberty. While I was working as a groupmother at St. Coletta School a young girl was enrolled. Soon after Arlene entered she had her first menstrual period. There was no problem at all because she had been carefully prepared by her mother. Arlene was spared all fear and embarrassment. She had everything needed and knew how to take care of herself.

Both boys and girls should be prepared for the developmental changes that take place, and they ought to be instructed about these changes in each other. Reverence for sex and respect for the human body can be inculcated at the same time that information is given. The consequent feeling of confidence provides a measure of security when sex becomes the center of interest among young companions. The individual who is developmentally disabled might be exposed to much that is cheap, lewd, and degrading, but will be less affected if he or she knows better and has a positive perspective.

For the developmentally disabled person, his/her handicaps will probably limit the choice in forming close relationships unless there are compensating qualities to make the boy or girl, young man or young woman, truly lovable. Profoundly and severely retarded individuals will lack the joys of marital relationship but will also be spared crucial responsibilities.

Down's syndrome individuals do have romantic ideas of boy friends and girl friends. At a benefit basketball game a lively young woman with Down's syndrome was seated in front of me. Each time one of the Milwaukee Bucks scored a basket, Roberta threw her arms into the air and shouted, "I'm going to marry him! I'm going to marry that one!"

There are to my knowledge twenty-four recorded instances of a female with Down's syndrome giving birth to a child. Approximately half of the babies had Down's syndrome and half were free of this condition. I am acquainted with no record of a male person with Down's syndrome ever fathering a child.

Greater concern centers about young people who are moderately or mildly affected by some form of disability. Learning to be their best selves—decent, honest, sincere, kind, self-respecting—forms an integrity that is its own reward. Single life can be a free choice, or it might be induced by economic or social circumstances. Young people who are mentally handicapped need to understand that many others are not able to marry for a variety of reasons.

A counselor discussed the question of marriage with several young people in the St. Coletta Training Center. In regard to their inclination to marry or not to marry, some of the responses were:

> "I shouldn't marry; I don't handle my own problems that well."

> "I wouldn't want to live with one person all my life."

> "I don't have to marry to live a satisfying life."

> "Maybe I'd like to get married so my Mom wouldn't have me to boss around anymore."

> "If I can find the right girl who would accept me with all my problems—"

> "Yes, because I like babies."

"No, because I wouldn't be able to support a family."

"No, because little kids get on my nerves; they cry too much."

"I'd worry about if my child would be normal; if my child would grow up would he accept me with all my problems?"

Serious dating is most frequently found among young people who have minimal brain damage or mild mental retardation. Training in wholesome leisure time activities offers outlets for boy-girl relationships in an open and enjoyable way. The greater freedom of recent years in working and playing together, with recognition of the spiritual component that monitors human relationships, promotes a healthful climate for dating and for the attraction of the opposite sex. Values form an important role in the sex education of a young person who is developmentally disabled. Sex properly used fosters a wholeness that is appropriate to the human person.

Young people who are handicapped need to be protected from contagion and other evils that attend promiscuity. A lifetime of intermittent pain and depression follows from allowing oneself to be sexually abused. Exposure to herpes and venereal diseases is a threat in these illicit relationships. Herpes simplex, a viral infection that presently has no cure and is commonly transmitted through sexual relations, now affects an estimated twenty million Americans, with a half-million new cases predicted annually. A counselor or advocate to advise and warn helps to safeguard young persons who may be eager for intimacy, but naive and confused about how to grow responsibly.

A personal relationship with Christ provides a sense of

value of being loved, even if the attempts at dating might be rejected. Most people have to deal with rejection at some time. It is important to value oneself, and to have faith in the abiding love of a Supreme Being who watches over and cares for those who trust in Him. Growth as loving persons is consistent with the plan of God. This growth develops lovable persons, pleasing to relate to and attractive to others. Developing beauty within is a step toward forming friendships. Caring persons can become popular in the true sense of the word. Again, choice is important: doing what is right rather than simply going along with others, especially if their ideals are less than desirable.

Like all people, the young person who is developmentally disabled does want to love and be loved. Recently as I came through the school corridor I met a glowing young woman who asked, "Do you know Jeff?"

"Yes, I know him." Both young people are trainees preparing for job placement.

"He's my boy friend. He gave me an engagement ring!"

I asked how she felt about this, and with an eloquent roll of her eyes, Carol replied, "Oh, he loves me, loves me very much!" I asked, "What are your plans?" Carol murmured, "I don't know."

Counseling is needed and is part of the program for these young men and women who are open to the thrills of intimacy but naive about choices to be made. Life is more than a body. The spirit, the soul, dominates in the choosing of a friend, one who may become a lifetime partner.

Greater regard for the dignity of handicapped persons among society in general will tend to safeguard the rights of those people who are limited, but human. Who is without limitations? All of us share with those persons who are developmentally disabled our own limits in creativity, achievement, and fulfillment of potential. They, in turn, share with all people the need to develop relationships, to enjoy social situations, and to be welcomed into wholesome activities.

Sex is not a separate department of life. It enters into the spiritual development of a human being. Christian educators, whether parents or teachers, need to encourage handicapped members toward a joyous sharing in companionship, giving affection in ways that are tender, caring, and appropriate in expression.

Feeling comfortable in a situation results when two or more people have interests and ideals in common. Building a positive relationship takes time and effort as well as mutual attraction. Dishonesty in human relationships, such as playing games with another's affections, will quickly spoil the chances of establishing genuine rapport.

Rather than steady dating with one individual, time should be spent in making a number of friends. Dangers of undue intimacy are avoided. Each relationship is a learning experience that provides growth toward maturity. Many wholesome group activities give enjoyment while individuals are getting to know each other better. Equally advantageous are group activities that include developmentally disabled persons with those who are free from noticeable handicaps.

The director of Coletta-James group home for young women, Madison, Wisconsin, shares guidelines for dating:

1) These women who are developmentally disabled, ages 20 to 31 years, have a right to date.

2) We expect the women to conduct themselves within acceptable standards of society and of our own household. Often we find that we must teach them behaviors that are usually taken for granted.

3) We need to provide structures and procedures to assist them in using good judgment.

4) We discuss appropriate places to meet new people, such as at work, at recreational activities and through other friends. We discourage forming acquaintances on the street or while riding buses.

5) We expect the young women to know basic information about a new boy friend, such as full name, where he lives, where he works, his age and marital status.

6) We try to make the women feel that their friends are welcome here to visit, for dinner, to watch TV, and to enjoy recreational activities.

7) We strongly request that staff members meet male friends before the women go out with them.

8) We recommend that dating be limited to daytime and early evenings. Movies, restaurants, walks, and sporting events are preferable to bars and visiting in apartments. We prefer the use of buses or walking to private cars.

9) The women are encouraged to go in groups, to pay their own way, to assert themselves and their decisions rather than to let the men handle everything. However, when a man invites a girl for a date, he should pay the bill.

The women at this group home are locally employed. While gaining experience toward independent living, it is essential that they also learn appropriate skills for developing relationships with both men and women. As each of the residents has a different level of social skills, it is sometimes necessary to have more specific rules for one individual while being more relaxed with others.

At this point in their lives they need a variety of friends, both male and female. The question of engagement and marriage comes up, but their main focus at the present time is to develop skills for the future. Friendships formed now can be supportive as they focus their energies on the long term goal of independent living.

Managing the relationship of steady dating is a step toward marriage. The question of marriage for developmentally disabled persons leads to controversy. Marriage is a natural human right but is also a grave responsibility involving not only the couple but also the desire they may have for children.

Attraction to a specific person of the opposite sex is a starting point. Mutual love enriches life for each other but will be tested by time and the realities of daily living. Personal aspirations need to be integrated into the basic necessities of holding a job, earning enough to maintain a home or apartment, and providing not only for the usual household expenses but also for emergencies such as health care.

Developmental disability may be of a type that is not transmitted to the children, but this apparently favorable fact can present its own problems. If the child is normal, will the home environment stimulate optimal mental growth? As the child develops, will there be acceptance of parental disabilities? If the child, or children, should also be defective, can special care and education be provided? Will the warmth of love be sufficient to give consistent security to the family unit?

Each time there is a question of marriage, guidance is needed in reviewing individual qualities and circumstances. Usually the right to marry presumes the right to have children. Counseling of young people who are developmentally disabled may lead to mutual agreement that procreation and upbringing of children is not advisable for them. Self-restraint in the enjoyment of sexual relations is one form of conception control, but other means are frequently advocated for developmentally disabled people. Some of these are offensive, others are morally objectionable, and still others are pastorally endorsed when weighing the values involved.

Compulsory sterilization is greatly resented by some handicapped individuals who want to have a child and who see this involuntary operation as an infringement of their rights. Young women upon whom this procedure has been forced feel wounded in terms of self-esteem, and see themselves as less women because of sterilization. While being sterilized prevents conception it does not protect from venereal disease, from rape, or from other forms of abuse.

Normalizing progress has been made since the time when institutional segregation kept developmentally disabled men and women apart. They were housed in dormitory buildings remote from each other, possibly sharing some recreational facilities but always under strict supervision. The heartache of being different intensified because of lack of freedom for satisfying friendships. Signs of sexual interest were ruthlessly repressed as a danger to society. This cruelty has been replaced by advocacy of rights: the right to love and to be loved, in spite of handicaps.

Over-protection on the part of parents, hesitation in letting go and fear of taking a risk, affects the lives of some handicapped persons. The support of pastoral counseling helps to bridge the step from a sheltered past into an uncertain future. This uncertainty is not unlike that experienced by other young people who marry and begin life on their own. Follow-up service to meet problems as they arise offers strengthening support to those who must contend with personal handicaps in their relation to each other and to life situations. The success rate of these unions, under favorable circumstances, compares favorably with the marriage/separation/divorce ratio of modern society.

Marriage can foster maturity because emotional growth takes place in the experience of making choices and decisions on a partnership level. A young couple who had been students at St. Coletta School tell their story:

> I am writing to let you know that we are very happy. Tom and I (Renee) grew up at St. Coletta's and we dated during our high school years. We would exchange letters. Tom gave me a ring, and we were serious about marriage after we left. He kept asking his parents to give permission for him to marry me, and they did. We never really had understood how to have sex and I found out it wasn't bad after all to share your love that way and to be unafraid of it.
>
> Our courtship started when we were on the bike track. Tom always walked with me and never left me except when we got ready for meals and at night. It lasted until we were married on September 26, 1981.
>
> Marriage is a real responsibility and we both have to talk about our feelings to be able to get along with each other. We are like "best friends" and it's been almost two years now since we were married.
>
> We will not be raising children because of my health to consider. We have a dog to help break the loneliness I feel about Tom working all day. I help out, too, and help with the men when they need me to sample corn, turn on and off the grain dryer, and canning. I don't have a garden yet.
>
> Yes, you may use our names. Give our best from the "Royal couple" of St. Coletta's to all the students and staff! Love and prayers! Tom & Renee Greiner.

Tom and Renee are fortunate in having excellent family support in their married life with steady employment for Tom and a favorable living situation. Economic security, positive family relations, their own personal qualities and their growth in emotional maturity predict well for their future happiness. Tom and Renee seem to have the fidelity required for long term commitment and the sharing of all aspects of life in a marriage based on mutual love.

When considering marriage for a person who is developmentally disabled, these questions might be asked: "Which person?" and "How has this person been prepared for the difficult, demanding tasks that wedded life and parenthood demand?"

In response to the first question, comparative examples can be considered by naming four persons who are typical of four levels of mental retardation. Only the first person named, Mary, seems capable of marriage and parenting. The others, while deserving of adequate sex education and all the vocational guidance of which they are capable, do not seem eligible for marriage and should not be encouraged in that direction. Of the four persons mentioned, each has had sex education at home and at school consonant with his/her level of receptivity. Each is nineteen years of age.

Mary is mildly retarded. Her sex education, biological as well as socio-religious aspects of her sexuality, has been thorough to the same degree that her sisters had prior to their marriages. While it has not been easy for Mary to learn to chart her fertility, her mother has insisted that, should marriage and babies be in the future for Mary, there should be a data base for mutual discussions between Mary and her husband in regard to children. Doctors have ruled out probable genetic risks should Mary have a family.

There is an open relationship between Mary and her parents; also between Mary and her two married sisters. Mary

the kinds of sports and entertainment he can handle. Uncle Jim doesn't rule out marriage completely but he fears that Ron would become an unhappy parent and weak husband because of his poor judgment and failure in assuming responsibility. Most of the family agree with this assessment. They hope that in Uncle Jim's home there will be happy experiences where Ron can assist as baby sitter and in other ways, but not be responsible for a household.

Don has Down's syndrome, scores an IQ of 45–50 on most intelligence scales, and comes from a warm, sometimes pampering, family environment. He has just begun half-day work experience planned by the local public schools. Marriage and parenting are beyond limits for this lad, but Don seeks intimacy. He wants to belong to someone; he wants to be somebody!

Family ties are the keys to successful integration of the Rons and Dons of society into settings where they will live happy and productive lives. When the supportive family is lacking, the challenge of integration becomes critical. Sometimes the Church and its professional workers have become important allies in this integration. For example, in response to the chatter about girl friends and marrying, the Rons and Dons can be confronted by a priest friend of the family: "Why don't you do what I am doing—become a friend and helper to everybody, but married to no one?"

In short, it seems that the vocation of young people like Ron, Don, and Susan has been written into their lives with their intellectual limitations. If parents and care providers can interpret this vocation accurately, they will counsel young people to plan for the future in a realistic manner by suggesting attractive alternatives. They will refrain from promises such as, "You can marry when you're older," if marriage should not be recommended at any age.

The success stories of persons with mild mental retarda-

has been given ample opportunity to help her sisters in their child rearing and household tasks. Her sisters will be a warm, enabling support to help Mary when and if she marries. She talks about marriage while enjoying the companionship of friends, both male and female, but she concurs with her mother who warns her about not getting serious until she has a job, feels more mature and is independent.

Susan is at the other end of the continuum. She is seriously impaired mentally, cannot comprehend formal sex education, but will always need, for her fullest development, the comforting touch and caring hands of those who love her. Susan will not marry or bear children but she will need to be called by name and be encouraged to relate to others. Sometimes, especially in institutional settings, the form of response may be modified and the response itself delayed. Never should the call for affection which Susan gives forth be rejected or denied.

Ron and *Don* rank between the mild retardation of Mary and the severe retardation of Susan, with moderate levels of developmental disability and questionable capacity for marriage/parenthood. Two levels of capacity typical of this group are described:

Ron has brain-damage and a score of 65 on the Binet test. He has been a high achiever, realizing his potential so that he has learned to read at 4.0 grade level. Ron is clever with his hands and speaks well. Both at home and in school he has received appropriate sex education. During his teen years Ron has had summer work on his Uncle Jim's farm. Ron saw among the animals "the miracle of life" his mother told him about. When he leaves school at age twenty, Uncle Jim will take Ron on as a hired hand on the farm.

Ron talks of his girl friends and of marriage. Uncle Jim is fearful that this talk might alarm the neighbors. He encourages Ron, for the present, to find his joy with the family and in

tion who have married, as well as the successful alternative choices of their less capable classmates, support the discernment suggested above. Accounts of these successes provide a warning lest we be too ready or too cautious when faced with the question of marriage/parenting for persons who are developmentally disabled.

Jean Vanier, writing under the title, "Love Is Being Together," says:

> We must consider what marriage means to handicapped people. For many, it is the mark of attaining adult status. Very many of the adults they know, starting with their own parents, will be married. So being married comes to mean being free, being adult, being recognized as a person.... And then there is the celebration. The man is the hero and the girl is the star. There are presents and champagne and special clothes. For the first time in their lives, perhaps, they are the most important people at the feast.
>
> ... The desire for marriage means the desire for happiness—the Kingdom of God is likened to a marriage feast.... Fulfillment lies on the other side of the marriage feast and wanting to get married is wanting to live in a world of peace and joy and belonging.

A holistic approach to sex education prepares the young person for crisis situations. In the lives of all people, crises can be expected to occur. Individuals with developmental disability are less vulnerable when prepared to accept positive values in relation to sex and to live by them.

8 *Crisis Situations*

An early crisis arises in a family and home with the birth of a child who is recognizable as developmentally disabled. After the mother's pain of childbirth, relief and joy gives way to anguish if the baby lacks the normalcy expected in a newborn child. During this crisis the parents need to give themselves time to realize that the infant is their special child, needing their love and care during helpless infancy.

One mother told me she left the hospital feeling that the Down's syndrome baby she took home with her was no more than a vegetable. There was no one to answer the questions that seemed to tear her apart. Long afterward she said that if the doctor had told her that these children are not complete losses, as her own child now grown to young womanhood has proved, she would have been spared months of mental and emotional torture.

The baby was easy to care for, but so strong was the mother's resentment that she hated to touch the child. Giving the baby a bath was pure agony as she struggled with the thought that suffocation in the water could look like an accident. This mother also battled with a temptation to turn on the gas jets in the kitchen to end her own desperation. She could not, however, cast aside a lifetime of training and belief. Accordingly, with the hope that some future time would bring healing, she persevered from day to day. In the meantime the baby was growing strong and healthy, enjoying her swing and outdoor naps. The father had accepted and loved her as if she were perfect, and she adored him. His understanding and support helped the mother as she grew to love her little girl even while resenting the retardation. I believe this shows the real dilemma, often ongoing, where a parent alternates between love for and rejection of a child who is developmentally disabled.

The parents of Joe, previously mentioned, had to wait until he reached eleven months before they received the diagnosis they had been asking for during the preceding months. Baby Joe had been hospitalized five times for asthmatic bronchitis, so this was given as the reason for his slow development, until finally they heard the diagnosis: mental retardation with minor physical anomalies. The specialist advised "Take him home and love him," but recommended that they consider placement in a state institution for the future. Information was meager but the parents shared what they knew with their four older children.

A visit to a state colony overwhelmed and discouraged them because they wanted Joe to reach his full potential. Gradually they met other parents who were sharing similar crises as they looked for the help they needed. One mother shared the theory she had adopted: "Don't push your child and don't discipline him—he can't learn anyway." So they didn't, and he didn't!

This mother did invite Joe's parents to accompany her on a visit to St. Coletta School where she went for an interview. Joe's mother says: "I was deeply impressed with what I saw there—the cleanliness, the disciplined compassion of the staff, and the outgoing personalities of the retarded people I met! That visit, before Joe was two years old, changed the whole course of his life."

The parents returned home with determination to get all the help they could toward Joe's development. They were given literature and read eagerly, then started a portable library for parents and became active in the Association for Retarded Citizens. When they tried to get local programs started they found that too many were satisfied with the idea, "Love 'em and let 'em be!"

For many parents the crisis gains momentum when their developmentally disabled child is ready for school. If placed in a special class or school, there is the probability of the child's being labeled "mentally retarded." Without the label, special educational services may not be available. Mainstreaming offers placement in the regular classes; if more help is needed, the twenty-four hour program of a residential school presents an option.

Placement at St. Coletta's or another residential school can itself produce a crisis. Unless preparation has eased the parting, the child feels uprooted from home and wonders why. Anger, grief, and insecurity mingle as he questions whether his parents care about him, whether they love him enough to know how he feels, or whether he is just being punished. One teenage boy took a neighbor's bicycle without asking, and went for a ride. An accident occurred, the bike was wrecked, and soon after this his turn came for admission to a residential school. An insight into his difficulty of adjustment was given when he asked another boy, "What did you do to get sent here?"

A former student, now independently employed, tells of his feelings at leaving home and family:

> A form of sorrow in my life was the first day I came to St. Coletta's. This happened on September 2, 1970. I had to leave my hometown to go to St. Coletta School to get a decent education for me. I cried very hard that day because my parents went home and I was left at St. Coletta's. I had a tough time for at least two years to get used to the program, but when I came there I decided not to let this sorrow bother me. I decided to get on with it and get down to learn the basic skills needed for my life.
>
> During my ten years in the school program and one

and one-half years in the Training Center, learning these skills was sometimes fun and sometimes frightening. I had to learn how to get along with my peers, teacher and group parents.

The situation for a child away at school is also difficult when there is trouble in the home: problems leading to the separation of husband and wife. Sometimes a child is placed in a residential school and the parents are divorced soon after the placement. A bewildered child wonders if he is the cause of the separation. Divorce can be as agonizing for a child as the death of a parent. It is natural to worry, "Who will take care of me?" or "Is it my fault?"

Since a divorce in a family seems as tragic as a death, it is important to get the feelings of a developmentally disabled dependent out into the open. When they are expressed, these feelings of sorrow, anger, guilt, insecurity, and a variety of mixed emotions can be dealt with through counseling. Showing pictures of persons whose faces show emotional strain and asking the individual to tell a story about the pictures helps a child to verbalize suppressed feelings. Suggesting the drawing of a picture and then telling the story of the drawing also helps to bring painful feelings to the surface where they can be dealt with.

At the transition from childhood and youth to early adult living there are new crises to face. Leaving school and entering the competitive world of work can be traumatic. During this period, coping successfully depends much upon adequate preparation.

Habilitation programs preparatory to job placement need to be realistically work-oriented with incidental academic supplements. For example, clients who lack the ability to measure, to tell time, to count money and make change, depend upon specific help in developing these skills based on number values. Tutoring sessions permit concentration on those areas most essential to the clients' needs.

Primarily, however, the training program must be directed toward personal qualities. Consistently acceptable behavior, emotional maturation, sense of responsibility and social growth are developed together with work skills, dependable habits, and those interpersonal relationships that are essential to getting and holding a job. Such qualities as foresight, initiative, judgment and will power may be minimal and need to be fostered under mature guidance.

Since the essence of a training program such as that offered at St. Coletta School is job training and eventual job placement, assigned work stations need close supervision. For beginners all work is on campus and includes such areas as food service, maintenance, teacher's aide, nurse's aide, clerical work, office practices, carpentry and farming. This early experience is followed by part-time or full-time jobs in the local community to give practice in competitive employment while still living at the school. Cottages a short distance from the main campus serve as transition houses for clients preparing for the move into independent living and self-support. At the cottages counselors are available on a twenty-four hour basis.

Guidance is given in all areas pertaining to adult living, but the real test comes when each young man or young woman moves into a job situation and probably into an apartment, either alone or with one or two companions. Follow-up service after job placement helps to avert crisis situations in regard to money management, but also in the appalling loneliness which some developmentally disabled persons feel even while they relish their new independence. Those are fortunate who have special interests or hobbies to occupy their leisure time during solitary hours or with companions from a peer group. At crucial times the support of a peer group eases the terrible feeling of aloneness that might confront a developmentally disabled person.

Some developmentally disabled young people suffer most because their mental level is high enough that they recognize its limitations. They realize that they do not have the freedom and privileges of normal brothers and sisters. Their rate of success is at a marginal level. Loss of job, being fired, inability to find employment or to give satisfaction when hired, can be so depressing that suicidal tendencies develop. If the feeling of failure is complicated by a broken home or loss of parental support, strong advocacy is needed to avert disaster. A caring situation, in which to touch base and get support, will help to bridge these times of crisis.

Sorrow brings a crisis into the life of a handicapped person as it does for all people who lose a loved family member or friend in death. If it is the loss of a parent in the early childhood of a developmentally disabled individual, the entire life situation is affected. During the early years of dependency, this child has a special need for the care and attention that loving parents provide. In each instance, the grief and forlorn feeling of loss calls for empathy. Telling over and over again, "My mother died," or "My mother went to heaven," seeks for someone to listen and to reflect the child's pain with a healing touch.

In this book my greater concern is for the adult handicapped person who must deal with sorrow. A former St. Coletta student, now successfully employed at a restaurant-theater and living independently, tells his own story of personal grief:

> When my Dad died it didn't come as a complete shock to me. I knew his cancer wasn't curable. When Dad was in the hospital it was very hard for me to see my

father in so much pain so I went to one of the nurses and asked, "How long will my father be able to live?" The nurse said, "He has only about four to six weeks to live."

After she told me that I went into the lounge and started to cry. While I was crying one of the nurses came up to me and gave me a big hug with a good understanding of what I was going through. The nurse told me that my father knew what I was going through, so after that I stopped crying and went back into my Dad's room. I had a beautiful conversation with him.

When Dad had cancer he took the pain rather well. He was the type that didn't get mad nor complain. He was very brave and I am proud of him. During my last conversation with Dad, it was a beautiful moment. I said, "Dad, if I don't see you again, please have this gold cross as a sign that our Lord Jesus is with you through this painful time in your life." I told him I got this cross at the St. Coletta Mission Sale.

I also said, "Please know that I, your son, love you always and I thank you for all the good times we shared together. I promise to take good care of Mom if you're not with us. I promise to keep on being a good son as I always have. If you leave us, say hello to everyone in heaven for us, including my grandparents. Please pray for us and remember us always."

Dad said, "Jim, you've been a great son. I'm proud of you. Please be a good boy as you always have been. Take good care of your mother. Let her know you're there with your support."

Before I left the hospital, I gave my Dad another hug and I said, "Father, I love you! Please remember me in heaven," and he said, "Yes, I will, and I love you, too." After that I left the hospital feeling sad but strong enough to realize that I had to go back and finish my training at St. Coletta's.

Soon after I went on a camping trip to Lake Wisconsin with the St. Coletta Boy Scouts . . . On Sunday, March

29, when the scouts and I started packing up to leave, I got a message from the scoutmaster. Mr. Arndt said, "Jim, your father died today."

After the announcement Mr. Arndt gathered all the scouts and held a small prayer service in the cabin for my family. After the prayer service I went for a walk with former scout leader, Mr. Thomas Link. During the walk, Mr. Link said, "Jim, if you feel like crying it's all right." I cried and while I cried I looked up to the sky and the sun was shining up there. Mr. Link said, "Jim, I understand how you feel. Your father was a good man. He was a good person to me as well as you and I will always remember him."

While I looked up at the sky I stopped crying and began to realize that he's up where the sunshine is. After the walk, Mr. Link and I both returned to the cabin to finish packing our camping gear and return as soon as possible so I could pick up and go home that same evening. On the way back, I sat in the front seat of the bus with Mr. Link. I looked out the window and observed the beautiful scenery of Wisconsin . . . and then I turned and thanked Mr. Link and the scouts for understanding how I felt. The scout leaders offered to come to the funeral in St. Paul so Mr. Lawrence . . . asked me to call.

When we arrived back at school, I was dropped off at St. Conrad Cottage to unpack my scout gear and pack my suitcase to fly home. Shortly after that Sr. Mary Jeanne, training center counselor, along with former habilitation clients, Mark Aspan and John Roth, came to the Madison Airport with me. It really meant a lot to me that evening with their presence there as friends. It gave me a sense of being understood and that I have a lot of friends who do care. It was raining hard that evening but fortunately my plane got off the ground on schedule and I arrived in my home town, St. Paul, Minnesota, safely. My brother John picked me up that evening.

The next day I went over to the funeral home and

witnessed my father lying in the casket. I knelt down and prayed to him. While at the funeral home it wasn't only a sad occasion but it was an occasion of belonging to friends who did understand. I felt happy to see some people whom I hadn't seen for many years. This occasion made me feel that after someone dies, there are still people who do care and do love you.

The next day was his funeral and the burial. At this occasion, I was asked to read the first and second readings. When asked to do this, I felt very honored and I felt it would make my father very happy and pleased. After the funeral Mass, my family and friends went to witness the burial of my father at National Cemetery, Bloomington, Minnesota.... My family drove in a limousine. I sat in the back with Mom and my younger sister Barbara. My sister and I sat very close to Mom to give her hugs to let her know that we're here in her time of grief and we love her. At the burial, it was a sad occasion but a beautiful one. Over Dad's casket was the American flag because Dad served as captain in the United States Marines. After the burial, the carriers presented my mother with Dad's flag, and then Mom wanted me to have it. She said Dad wanted me to have it because I've served in Boy Scouting. When I got the flag, I felt very honored, thankful, and I felt happier.

After the funeral I stayed home for a few days and then returned to St. Coletta's and was happy to be back. I had to realize that I must go on and live my life as my father wants me to live. After Dad's death, some prayers were answered. The first prayer was for me to have a job where I'm happy, busy, and close to my friends whom I grew up with at St. Coletta's. I got a job at the Fireside Restaurant in Fort Atkinson, Wisconsin. I said in prayer, "Thanks, Dad! Thank You, God!"

The second prayer was answered six months after the first prayer. I moved into an apartment with two former

St. Coletta students. Since then, I've been doing well on my job and in my apartment.

I want to say that time heals wounds. I realize that when someone close to you dies, there will always be someone there who loves and cares about you. The minute before Dad died, his last words to Mom were, "Take care of my Jim." When Mom told me this I was very happy. I still miss Dad but his sweet memories will always be treasured in my heart.

Jim's father died after a comparatively brief illness. The mother of George, a resident worker, had been in poor health for forty-six years, even before George was born with spastic cerebral palsy. His father died while George was an infant. When George was eleven years old he learned that he had had a brother and a sister, both of whom died within a few hours after birth. George, now forty-one, says:

My mother met my second father in 1955. She brought him here to visit on Easter Sunday and again on Mother's Day. She said they would be married on July 12, but I think they were already married although I can't prove it. One nice thing they did for me was to let me go to Europe in 1960, three years before my dad died.

In 1977 I was very disappointed because I wanted to have that last Christmas with my mother. I couldn't, because she was too sick. I knew she was going to die. I felt sorry when my mother died but . . . one thing I realize, now that my mother is gone, is how much she loved me. I don't think we realize while they are living how much our parents love us.

These accounts show that sorrow and death are part of life for developmentally disabled persons just as they are for other people, and the feelings are much the same. One of

George's comments was: "My mother had to suffer and I have to suffer, too." Only human beings can find meaning in their pain, and in this regard George shows his humanness even if handicapped. He bears pain with dignity, convinced that his life is worthwhile. The meaning of death is related to life, reflecting the happy days, the good times, as well as the days that were shadowed by loneliness, sorrow or pain.

Another type of crisis occurs when the developmentally disabled person in some way goes astray and comes into conflict with the law. Empathy and help are needed as seen in a review of these situations in the next chapter.

9 Conflict with the Law

Many forces exert influence on the patterns of conduct formed by a person who is developmentally disabled. The pressure of companions, the often erotic lessons from the media, the frustrations of failure and of feeling different—all have their effects. If parents have done their best to direct the development of good character in their child, and still the individual gets into trouble with the law, these parents should not torment themselves, saying, "Where were we wrong? What should we have done differently?"

Problems of anti-social behavior in early childhood may be the first steps that lead a person who is developmentally disabled into conflict with the law. Problem behavior is usually a symptom of maladjustment which disturbs the emotional life of a young person. Uncorrected misconduct sanctions repetition of the behavior.

Neglected behavior leads to delinquency. Consistency in handling behavior problems is the key to a well balanced sense of right or wrong. Parental reactions to a child's misconduct must be in harmony from one day to the next. Because individuals who are developmentally disabled lack ability for subtle distinctions, there is an increased obligation to clarify for them the difference between behavior that is approved and that which is unacceptable.

There comes a certain time in every person's life when this person must take responsibility for his/her behavior. With increased respect for the rights of persons who are developmentally disabled, there is also increased accountability. They cannot place all blame on their parents for what they do. Good parents try their best but cannot exclude other influences.

Unless discipline becomes self-discipline it has little permanent value. The attempt to forestall misbehavior through fear of punishment loses its effect when the threat is removed. Good habits have the strongest hold on an individual when he sees them lived by those he loves. Love is the greatest motivating force in life and a child who feels himself unloved is prone to delinquency. Reading the sad accounts of juvenile delinquents and adult criminals causes one to question whether these persons ever experienced the warmth of a loving relationship.

Were they abused as children? Did they learn to fear and to hate those persons who should have given them loving care? Was their early environment cold and hostile? Were they punished and humiliated by teachers because they couldn't learn at a normal rate? Were they rejected by peers who saw that they were different? Were they so anxious to please, to get attention, that they became tools of unscrupulous deviates who caused them to become victims of legal procedures, while the real criminals escaped the punishment decreed by law? If so, they were probably individuals with developmental disability. The handicapped person, often starving for attention at any price, is easily exploited and incapable of self-defense.

Some persons with developmental disability need protection because they are not able to understand the restrictions of the law. Marijuana and other drugs that cannot be exchanged openly might involve a handicapped go-between in deep trouble, about the danger of which he may be utterly unaware. I read the account of one father whose retarded son had been misused in this way and was then arrested. In a fury the father attacked the evil agent who was gloating over his newly acquired wealth, gained through betraying a naive youth into having a criminal record. The father's anger, righteous as it was, backfired because he, too, was arrested; his offense: violent assault.

The person who is developmentally disabled finds himself in a minority with a unique problem. Laws are written for the average person. Providers of legal service and of criminal justice or retribution often are lacking in their understanding of persons who are mentally retarded. Bias and prejudice against these people with handicaps may prevent sensitivity to their limitations and special needs.

As the move to deinstitutionalize marginal people becomes prevalent, more of those who are mentally retarded will be in positions where weak insight into situations and failure to foresee consequences spell trouble. Not knowing "the difference between mine and thine" can lead to arrests for stealing. Wanting things they do not have money to buy may lead to shoplifting. Outbursts of anger when malicious teasing goes beyond endurance can cause acts of violence. Sometimes the very openness of unself-conscious behavior (e.g., masturbation, indecent exposure, or trespassing on private property) leads the naive person to offend, whether or not any serious civil law is broken.

The use of behavior modification has emerged as a promising approach for instilling acceptable behavior. Reinforcing the desirable behavior with approval helps the individual to discriminate acceptable from objectionable habits of conduct. This training is preventive by nature and can begin early in life. Equally important is the training of personnel in the criminal justice system to identify individuals who are mentally retarded, to know their limitations and to understand how they function. This training could save persons who are handicapped from being unduly prosecuted, tried, and convicted when not guilty of a crime.

A study by Brown and Courtless indicated that of

200,000 persons in correctional institutions in 1971, ten percent, or 20,000, would have some degree of mental retardation. A more recent study indicates that the percentage varies according to the geographical region of the country, probably because developmental disability is more frequent in heavily populated, poverty-stricken areas.

An officer who notices defects of speech, deficiencies in intelligent response, and sometimes lack of identification such as a driver's license or credit cards may suspect probable mental retardation. Escorting the person home and checking with parents or guardians would help to safeguard the individual's legal rights.

If arrested, a person with mental retardation may easily be coerced into pleading guilty. Confessions then result from suggestion or intimidation rather than from actual guilt. Resource persons who understand developmental disability can help to prevent our prisons from an over-population of innocent, defenseless persons.

In "An Essay on the Legal Rights of the Mentally Retarded" (*Family Law Quarterly*, 1972), Haggerty, Kane and Udall tell of a young mother accused of poisoning her child by putting arsenic in the infant's formula. A lawyer questioned her at length and felt he had complete knowledge of his client. Another attorney present at the hearing noticed signs of retardation and asked the client three questions: Could she find her mother's telephone number in the directory? Could she count a handful of change? Could she add twenty-four and twenty-four? She was absolutely unable to do any of these tasks. This attorney, the father of a child with mental retardation, was fortuitously qualified to disclose more insight in a brief interview than the other lawyer learned in ninety minutes of questioning. Because her retardation was brought to the attention of the judge, this young mother was sent to a state school for women of child-bearing age instead of being sentenced to jail.

Law enforcement personnel need information that will help them to see the offender who is mentally retarded as differentiated from the offender who is normally intelligent. The officer is then able to better protect the rights of the retarded person as well as those of society. Even when the accused person with mental retardation is advised of the right to keep silent, to refuse to answer questions without consultation with an attorney, it is likely that he will not fully comprehend these privileges. Because of his retardation, the suspected person is apt to yield either to threats or to friendly advances designed to induce cooperation.

In case of an arrest, it is equally important that the authorities concerned be aware of the difference between an offender who is mentally retarded as contrasted with one who is mentally ill. Psychiatric attention is required for the person who is mentally ill and, therefore, not competent to stand trial. For the suspected offender who is mentally retarded, the problem is a lifelong handicap rather than a temporary problem offering promise of remediation. It is possible that a person who is mentally retarded may also be mentally ill, but the two conditions require different treatment appropriate to each.

There is grave injustice if the offender who is mentally retarded or developmentally disabled is sent to an institution for those who are considered criminally insane. The person who is retarded requires protective custody for his own sake, and also if there is danger to society. The degree of probable danger would determine whether there is need for full custody or whether life at home under supervision of parents or guardian will meet the need. Adapting procedures and programs to the needs and capacities of an individual offender will help to prevent a cycle of recidivism.

The offender who suffers from poverty as well as limited mental capacity may have the least chance for helpful consideration. Also, court appointed lawyers can be overloaded with indigent clients, or there is likely to be a lack of appropriate correctional facilities and treatment programs. An individual who is economically deprived may also have been a victim of neglect or child abuse. School failure, truancy, poor self-concept and weak self-control tend to aggravate the effects of poverty.

Prejudice based on the idea that persons who are developmentally disabled lack moral sense, or have a tendency toward criminal pursuits, may cause bias in the arresting officer. His ability to communicate without a negative approach could be a crucial step in the proper handling and rehabilitation of the retarded client. This positive attitude is also essential in dealing with the parents. A barrier may result from their guilt feelings, sense of frustration, and anxiety over a family member in conflict with the law.

In interviewing the parents, an officer needs to realize the traumatic effect of having a handicapped son or daughter arrested for breaking the law. He is dealing with a crisis situation in the family. Even when carefully explained, the procedures in which they find themselves entangled are complex. Some parents, having mental limitations of their own, will feel confused over these complexities. Counseling can save them from being overwhelmed by the situation facing them and their child. The problem might not be solved, but counseling is helpful to relax tension and relieve the burden of anxiety while the issue is being resolved. The retarded offender should be permitted to share with the parents in these sessions as a protection against the panic of feeling himself excluded from their concern. Basically, this individual needs a simple, clear-cut interpretation of his problem and of the appropriate conduct required at the time and place.

Persons who are developmentally disabled need specific guidance rather than punishment. Many of their actions, labeled as unacceptable behavior, are actually fear reactions in unfamiliar, frustrating, or tempting situations. Because an adult who is mentally retarded presents different problems than a person with normal intelligence, there is need for the understanding that helps to develop a feeling of dignity and self-respect. Without this strengthening of the self-concept, rehabilitation of the retarded offender fails to achieve its goal. Behavioral change from within is more effective than external control.

Developmental disability, conflict with law, correctional procedures: each of these presents complex problems. Police officers, lawyers and judges benefit when they seek in-service training to become knowledgeable regarding characteristics that identify individuals as being mentally disabled or retarded. Suspected offenders who are retarded but able to stand trial need pretrial information that will help them to understand better the criminal justice system. Shortage of services for accused persons who are mentally retarded implies the risk that inability to understand, to think quickly, and to communicate clearly is likely to deter justice when developmentally disabled persons are concerned.

From among the many young people with developmental disability who have gone into independent living and employment after leaving the Training Center at St. Coletta School, there are several incidents of conflict with the courts of law. One young woman was invited to a wedding reception on a Friday evening. Here she met a young man who took her to his home while the parents were away for the weekend. He kept her in the basement and raped her repeatedly before releasing her on Sunday evening. The girl did not know his name but was able to point out the house. She was advised to prefer charges because of the traumatic assaults against her person. However, the district attorney recommended that she should not do so. The young man of normal intelligence was only seventeen years old. Since she was twenty-one the law would not be in her favor—she could, therefore, be convicted for contributing to the delinquency of a minor.

In another incident, a solicitor who was selling magazines came to an apartment and induced the resident, a young woman with developmental disability, to sign for about two hundred dollars' worth of subscriptions. The girl was a non-reader, and her earnings were not sufficient that she could afford any magazines. However, the contract was considered valid and she would be held responsible for payment. Then an advisor from St. Coletta's examined the contract and found that it was dated February 29 although this was not a leap year. The inaccuracy of the date did invalidate the contract. There had been no provision for canceling subscriptions, and the girl had been influenced by a handsome young man who gave her attention. Signs were soon placed at the various apartments prohibiting all solicitation.

One young man got into trouble as a "peeping Tom," looking into windows of residences during early morning hours in the town where he was employed. People of the town were dismayed. Because they were worried, he was obliged to leave his job and return to his home state or charges would be pressed against him.

In another instance where a young man was suspected of a serious misdemeanor, the district attorney insisted that charges be pressed and his guilt verified in court. Only through being convicted could the young man receive the help of a treatment program at a correctional facility. Had he gone free, he would probably have developed a life of criminal conduct; had he gone to jail, he would not have been provided the rehabilitation his developmental disability required.

Another incident was handled with less discretion. The unfortunate circumstance occurred when a girl who was inclined to be promiscuous disappeared from her job and went with a truck driver to a distant state. When she reappeared, pregnant, she named a former client from the training center as father of the child. He was employed at a considerable distance and had moved to a new place of residence within the same town. Consequently, the summons to appear in court never reached him. One morning as he was going to work a police car drew up to him. He was handcuffed and driven seventy-five miles without any explanation. Upon arrival at police headquarters he was thrown into jail until the following Monday. He was not prepared to make a telephone call although this privilege was offered to him. When he appeared in court and heard the charges he denied them vehemently. Blood tests proved his innocence. When he asked how to get back to his place of work and what explanation to give his boss for the days of absence, he was told, "That's your problem, buddy." After this callous response he hitchhiked the seventy-five miles back to his place of employment. Developmentally disabled, he had been subjected to several days in jail, confined with drunkards and other miscreants awaiting trial.

Another young man on his first job became involved with the selling of marijuana. He was given an option of going to jail or accepting "house arrest" under strict supervision for thirty days. He chose the latter option, became docile, and established controls over his own behavior which had never before conformed to controls. He now has a new job and is doing well. In this instance the lawyers and judge considered mental age in adapting laws that were written according to chronological age.

Alcoholism also presents problems when a worker who is mentally retarded spends his earnings in a tavern. Fear of losing one's job is a deterrent for those who like beer but want to have a satisfactory work record. Return to the training

After outlining recommendations for action, Johanek expresses a concluding plea:

> ... we are still afraid to reach out to one another, to hear the cry of the imprisoned, to touch the hurt heart of another human being. If we are alive, then we must respond to life—all life—not just life on this side of the bars, not just life that is comfortable, but life that is giving to those who cannot choose life for themselves—those "different drummers" in our world.

The Handicapped Offender, a survey published by the National Criminal Justice Reference Service, concludes that there are proportionately more people with mental retardation in prisons and jails than in the general population. Estimates by prison experts indicate that the number in inmate populations ranges from nine percent nationally to as high as thirty percent in some states. The survey recommends that prison employees receive training in order to recognize offenders who are mentally handicapped and to develop programs for them. The young offender who is retarded becomes vulnerable to exploitation by inmates and staff unless protected. Provision for in-service training could help toward a better understanding and improved treatment for prisoners who are developmentally disabled.

Especially for juvenile delinquents who are mentally retarded, it is imperative that special educators cooperate with corrections personnel so that these young people will not join the ranks of adult prison inmates who had juvenile records. The zero reject principle is not met until services reach those individuals whose retardation may be part of the reason why they come into conflict with the law.

The American Catholic Correctional Chaplains Association was founded in 1952 by the bishops of the United States to keep the Church in the foreground for assistance to prisoners who, lacking freedom to seek spiritual sustenance, need to find healing while paying their debts to society. The duties of a prison chaplain are similar to those of the pastor in a parish—to administer the sacraments, to share the good news of the Gospel, and to minister to the spiritual needs of persons separated from normal living situations. The chaplain is in a unique position to establish relationships based on understanding and good will toward the spiritual nature of individuals in desperate need for the uplift of religion in their lives.

Prison Fellowship, founded by Charles W. Colson after his own incarceration, aims toward new life for forgotten prisoners through a personal relationship with Jesus Christ. Colson recognizes that He alone offers a solution to the crime problems that plague our nation. Prisoners who are spiritually rehabilitated then become a leaven for others. Quoting one of them:

> To me, Prison Fellowship has been a vessel of God's love—a shining light. It has been Jesus' love in action. These volunteers have walked the extra mile with me and helped make my burden lighter. They have shared my hurts and frustrations, as well as my joy. Every one of them has been a rare gem of a friend—the kind that are hard to find. Through them, I have come to know the love of Jesus Christ. (*Newsletter* of Prison Fellowship in Wisconsin, April 1983)

Since persons who are developmentally disabled are overrepresented in our penal system, they present a special challenge for religious ministry. Awareness of their spiritual needs, often clouded over by the prisoners' resentment toward the system, calls religious personnel to provide long-range, patient, perceptive healing. Like all persons, handicapped or whole, those in conflict with the law have an inherent need to be in touch with God.

10 *In Touch with God*

Christianity celebrates the triumph of the risen Christ by recognizing the worth of each human life, no matter how feebly it functions. Every person is gifted with an immortal soul, a breath of life from God Himself. Even the individual who is severely retarded has a greater value in the eyes of God than all the wealth of the mineral, vegetative, and animal kingdoms combined. This secret of intrinsic worth justifies every effort and expenditure which caring can direct toward the needs of persons who are developmentally disabled.

Regardless of the degree of disability, parents seek an assurance that the Church cares about their child. Caring is a part of religion, and this caring includes self as well as concern for others. An adequate self-concept centers about the conviction, essential to every person, "I am graced, loved, gifted, nurtured in the embrace of my family." Beyond this unit, the extended family of God's people gives the sense of mutuality, an interchange of caring and responsibility for each other.

Like every normal boy or girl, the child with mental retardation is a person sent by God for a unique purpose no other human being can accomplish. The prime purpose in life for every person tends to give glory to God by fulfilling His plan, a design that excels any humanly devised idea. This purpose can be attained by each created being according to individual capacity. The child, adolescent or adult who is developmentally disabled witnesses that, from person to person, this capacity varies greatly. In an intricate mosaic, some of the stones are brilliant and others are muted, but each shade and shadow contributes to the perfection of the whole.

The concept of personal worth and individual dignity is based on religious and ethical convictions. These form part of the theory of our democratic creed. From either viewpoint the inherent value of the human being is recognized. Developmentally disabled persons, therefore, are recognized as having God-given rights based on the dignity of their human personality endowed with an immortal soul. These rights entitle a handicapped person to be considered eligible for the best treatment that society can give a human being. In keeping with this thought are the following words of the late Cardinal Cushing of Boston: "It is not a problem of the lowness of the child's intellectual ability, but the highness of man's ability to serve that child."

Every person, and the one with mental retardation is no exception, has been fashioned by the Creator according to the image of God. This likeness applies particularly to the soul. Likeness to God implies a life of grace which is gained through baptism and preserved by choosing to do good and to avoid evil. The person who learns to recognize God as a most loving and perfect Father can choose to please Him. Thus the person, regardless of handicap, can increase his likeness to God by increasing the life of grace in his own soul.

Only God can measure this power of choice in relation to the strength or weakness of the human mind, but for each person there is an exact equation between his power and his potential. The likeness of God will reach relative perfection in the soul of each individual who uses his *all* for the glory of God and the good of his fellow men. A defective brain limits the functioning of the mind but it does not diminish the worth of the soul. In the same manner a broken string on a violin hampers the playing of an artist but it does not destroy his or her musical ability.

The gift of life is the first step toward eternal life. Parents have the satisfaction of knowing that they have made it possible for their son or daughter to achieve happiness. For parents with faith, the opportunity of sharing their religious heritage with each family member promotes inner serenity. Parents who are without religious convictions will find it harder to see meaning in, and to accept the daily struggle in, working with one of the most heartbreaking problems in life: the duty to provide full opportunity for a child with developmental disability.

In religious Christian schools the spiritual goal determines program planning for the child with special needs. The following schema combines the moral and the catechetical aspects while respecting psychosocial growth. Spiritual/moral awareness on the part of a child who is developmentally disabled progresses to adulthood, with its beginning at the earliest level of consciousness:

I—The idea of self-awareness, self-exploration, recognizing self as different from the rest of the world. At first, with the very young child, everything goes into the mouth. Then the little one subconsciously realizes "Mother and Daddy make me feel secure, wanted, cared for." The child then reaches out for the bigger world, the world of

WE—The child begins to realize that "My pleasure is not the only value. Others have rights and responsibilities and so do I. *We* can and must work together, e.g., you teach me how to tie my shoe and I'm much freer, but now I'm responsible to do it and I am invited to show another how to do it. Why is this?" Because the world is ordered by

GOD—Awareness of a God-ordered universe is a quantum step. The individual learns that "Now I have a *frame* for reality, for my own story, for all religious and moral development." This dawn of realization comes with growth in mental age and continues until the beatific vision. As a famous psychoanalyst (T. Reik) said, one moves from *my will be done* to *Thy will be done.* That is the work of a graced lifetime.

The individual begins to understand that "God does not want certain things because they are *not* good for me, even if I like them," e.g., "I should not eat too much, nor drink too much." God as a loving Father becomes personal to individuals as they learn to pray and give thanks. He gives His gifts and teaches how He wills them to be used through Holy Scripture. Persons who are developmentally disabled respond to Scripture as they learn that God has a special book, the Bible, which tells His people how to live and to love each other.

Parents and care-providers help the child to see that "a loving God wants me to love Him and to love others." God's law, the Ten Commandments, show many ways to

LOVE—These Ten Ways of giving love combine caring, sharing, and being responsible for one's life with God and with others. Choosing what is right becomes basic to all the ways of loving God and loving each other. Love is giving love, giving prayerful thanks to God.

Sister Coletta Dunn writes, "Here is the age-stage where I teach children to pray with their whole bodies in a prayer of thanks for *life*. I ask the child to love all those God has given us: parents, siblings, friends, helpers, teachers."

Love is *forgiving* love. Persons who are developmentally disabled frequently suffer hurt and rejection. Unless one learns to forgive, hurt feelings damage the self-concept and cause a person who is handicapped to become embittered by the abuse of others. Parents might help their child to say: "God loves me just as I am and He asks me to love all His other children, even the ones who are mean to me." The Christian finds powerful examples of forgiveness in

JESUS—Who was rejected but Who prayed for the forgiveness of those who hurt Him. In giving His example, Jesus could say, "I am the light of the world.... Whoever follows Me will have the light of life and will never walk in darkness." (John 8:12) The capacity to forgive brings light and joy while refusal to forgive leads to darkness and resentment.

Parents and care-providers can help the person who is developmentally disabled, through their own firmness of faith and love of Jesus, to understand that Jesus is the true Son of God Who saves His people from their sins and brings them to the enjoyment of His love in heaven. There are many ways in which Jesus can save His people, and He does this especially through His

CHURCH—The family of God who journey together with Him. From the concept of Jesus, the developmentally disabled person reaches out to the Church, the community Jesus established. Through the Church Jesus has a way of relating to an organized group of people devoted to God. Religion gives the sense of belonging, through Church membership, without which individuals who are handicapped become lonely persons.

All of Christian life from baptism to the Beatific Vision is a journey with Jesus. All persons, regardless of gifts or limitations, are invited to this journey. A "Yes" response to this invitation is most visible when Christians meet Jesus in the sacraments of the Church. The curriculum series *Journey With Jesus* (Cardinal Stritch College, Milwaukee) looks at religious instruction as a preparation for the sacraments of Holy Communion, Reconciliation, and Confirmation as a sign of belonging to God's Church. Sister Coletta Dunn, co-author of *Journey With Jesus,* explains:

> In the dialogue which God initiates with His people three rhythms stand out: His call to **Communion,** His call to **Reconciliation,** and His call to **Service.** As we study these calls we realize that our response depends upon how well we have learned to commune with Him, on how well we have learned to receive His gifts with grateful hearts, and on how well we have understood Christian service—from Mary's to ours. All these basic understandings constitute **Sacramental Readiness** for a Call to Communion, a Call to Reconciliation, and a Call to Service.
>
> More immediate preparation for sacrament is done on the level of instruction designated **Sacramental Preparation.** During this period the student for whom our lessons are designed is encouraged to enter more deeply into an understanding of Eucharistic Communion. He begins to celebrate Reconciliation, sacramentally, if he is capable. As he continues to understand his place in the Church, he studies the sign of that belonging—Confirmation.
>
> We believe that initiation to the sacraments is to be followed by intensive years of follow-up to enable the learning disabled person to understand and live sacraments. Excitement and/or confusion which often accompanies the first reception of the sacraments can yield to understanding when we provide a year of post-sacrament instruction. . . . Programs should respect the maturity of retarded adults while helping them gain spiritual benefit from each Sunday's Gospel. It is this group of spiritually neglected adults who desire the crumbs of the Gospel. They shall grow in wisdom and grace when the Bread of the Word and the Bread of the Eucharist are available to them. . . . This is the intent of our **Gospel Study** units.

The response of people who are developmentally disabled depends on how well they have learned to relate to Jesus in prayer, to receive His gifts with grateful hearts, and to understand their role in Christian service. Sacramental meetings with Jesus, participation in the liturgy, and services to others who share the journey help to mentally enrich the daily living of persons who are mentally handicapped.

To illustrate this enrichment, Sister Sheila Haskett, principal author of *Journey With Jesus,* shared the Gospel story of the rich man with aging residents at the Alverno Cottages for long-range personal care at St. Coletta School. In explaining the parable, Sister asked, "What does it mean to be rich? Are any of you rich?" Several persons indicated that certain individuals claimed to be wealthy, e.g., they had their own spending money; they had various personal treasures. One of the last to speak was Gloria, who said, "I am rich. I have Jesus in my heart."

Gloria's statement suggests that only in the realm of the spiritual can we grasp the problem of handicap. "Why did it happen?" has an answer hidden in the mystery of pain and suffering. The question we need to ask with the handicapped person is this: "How can I strive within the framework of my disability to become more fully a person? How can I use my handicap to give witness to the good news of Jesus?"

Religious living is a powerful means of maintaining mental health for individuals and for families. Suffering and deprivation are not good in themselves but only in the way they are interpreted and the use that is made of them. By working through painful struggles in faith, one achieves a spiritual strength that would not be there otherwise. The developmentally disabled person who has known the supporting, nurturing love of the family can find joy in the nurturing love of God. Family members who can forgive the limitations and mistakes of a person who is awkward in action and weak in judgment are helping this person to believe in God's loving forgiveness.

Parents need to remember that many of today's values are counter-Christian. Each person, whether handicapped or not, is called to embrace a value system. The Christian climate pervading a home is a means of bringing the "little ones" to Jesus. When family members enflesh the teachings of Jesus, an atmosphere of prayerfulness in the home prepares the child for wordless speaking with God long before a developmentally disabled person is mentally ready for formal prayer.

To serve the person who is handicapped it is necessary to serve the whole family. There is a choice, or combination of two goods: what is good for the individual and what is good for others, especially family members. Sister Sheila Haskett, speaking for families with whom she has worked, says in her Preface to the *Director's Handbook for Journey with Jesus,* ". . . a strong bond has developed among us. We have prayed together, shared our delights in the children, supported one another in times of grief and loss—in short, we have come to care about one another in a very special way. We have developed a sense of identity as a pilgrim band on our Journey with Jesus to the Father."

Developmentally disabled persons on this pilgrimage have known the charity and protection of Christianity during centuries when neglect and abuse were the common lot of underprivileged people. The universal message of God's love continues to be shared with people as they are, including those who live their lives under handicapping conditions. Long before a low IQ was identified, Jesus invited all to come to Him.

Special religious education begins in early childhood, in the home. As the child grows and develops, there is need for spiritual growth to keep pace. The need for spiritual nurture will never be outgrown. Promoting acceptance as a person, even when the person is severely handicapped, is a form of spiritual nurture that persists through adulthood. Meeting this need is one of the most humanly appealing services a Christian community can offer to its special members.

A person who is childlike mentally loves as a child: simply, sincerely, wholeheartedly. The capacity for spiritual growth reaches beyond the measure of intelligence. Offering religious education does help these persons to find joy in pleasing God through full development of their entire personalities. As every human individual is not only body but spirit also, there is an attraction to spiritual growth and eternal interests. God is love, and in His love the lives of persons who are developmentally disabled become worthwhile. As a way of life, religion directs all activities toward God with a consistent effort to do good and avoid evil.

Parents should not be too ready to assume that their son or daughter, limited by developmental disability, cannot learn moral values. Sometimes these children have a keen sense of what is right or wrong. Constant good example and careful explanations will strengthen this discrimination and foster right conduct. Insofar as the person understands, he or she can choose. On the other hand, unless "being good" is prompted by love, good behavior lacks its strongest motivation.

By their own integrity parents model behavior that helps to form a right conscience in the child who is developmentally disabled. The child learns far more from what the parent does than from directives given if these are not reinforced by good example. Parents who are honest, truthful, kind, fair-minded in dealing with others and observant of norms for right living set a pattern with which the child identifies more readily than through verbal instruction. Parents who become angry and upset over a mishap, such as accidental spilling or breaking, cause a sensitive child to feel greater guilt than over a misdeed that is morally wrong but lightly passed over.

Intelligence is a critical factor in the individual's responsibility for moral behavior. Persons who are profoundly retarded present no real problems in judging culpability. On the other hand, limited concept of the goodness or badness of an act is found in individuals with a mental age of three to seven years. Although they are capable of some moral training, their degree of responsibility is low. Lacking sufficient reflection, such youngsters fail to see the implications of their actions and to foresee consequences. Because they have no thought of anything beyond the immediate present, they bear no culpability for their action.

The handicapped adolescent or the adult with a mental age of seven years, the age designated for the awakening of moral consciousness, has a different degree of development than a seven-year-old child. Moral problems do arise with such individuals who are moderately or mildly retarded. Because reason so weakly guides his tendencies to seek good for himself and others, the person with mental retardation is rather easily misled if he becomes the tool of unscrupulous companions. Despite a mental level of a young child, the person may have the physical strength, the emotions and the impulses to commit serious misdeeds.

The degree of moral consciousness will vary with intelligence and training. Persons with mental handicap are able to love to the degree to which they have insight and also to hate in the same degree. Moreover, emotional experiences charged with significance are likely to affect the moral responsibility for their actions.

Conscience is the subjective norm for moral decisions and actions, implying freedom of the will and the use of reason, but bad example and false teaching sometimes form an erroneous conscience. Since conscience is the practical judgment of the moral goodness or sinfulness of an action, it must be correctly formed through proper training. Conscience is not ready-made, but each person has a natural inborn aptitude to grasp the main obligations of right living, e.g., an appreciation of the value of life, property, truth, and a certain reverence for parents and matters of sex.

If it were humanly possible to measure the degree of moral responsibility in developmentally disabled persons, the range would be from no responsibility for some individuals so severely retarded that they have the mental ages of infants, to almost complete responsibility for persons with mild retardation, favorable environmental influences, and excellent moral training. In between these two extremes the great majority of people with mental retardation would have varying degrees of reduced responsibility for their moral choices of behavior.

According to their mental levels, individuals who are developmentally disabled can be taught a system of values essential to right living. We can expect that it will take prolonged training to help them acquire a sense of true values. Good habits, once they are firmly established, are usually consistently followed. Conversely, it may take a long time to supplant bad habits with repeated good deeds. Therefore, a sound moral training early in life becomes immeasurably important.

Parental training sometimes inadvertently teaches improper values. In good faith, some parents try to make up for their child's handicap by granting every desire. Such indulgence makes the child self-centered. Problems difficult to solve result from a poor code of values. Evil tendencies can be overcome only with God's help through prayer with the understanding guidance and good example of those persons who care for the individual.

Institutional living presents problems for all persons, normal and mentally retarded alike. Generally speaking, staff members are unable to provide all the love and understanding necessary for emotional growth. The resulting deprivation may increase an urge to seek love in an inappropriate relationship. Moral problems then develop or existing disturbances accelerate. On the other hand, institutions do protect from many dangers and difficulties of unsupervised living. In doing so they may fail to develop an adequate sense of autonomy. An individual who feels secure while in the sheltered environment may feel lost and insecure when removed from the protective surroundings. In loneliness, the person is easily led to whoever will give time and attention. To safeguard moral integrity, vigilance balanced by opportunities to make choices and decisions is needed during the years in an institution or a residential school to prepare the individual for challenges of later life.

In a residential school not only the chaplain and teacher, but the group parents, too, like a mother/father in a home, realize responsibility toward the souls of the children. Spiritual, moral, and social growth must keep pace with educational progress. Preparation for life in its fullest sense is the primary concern for those entrusted with the care of others, even of those who are severely limited.

Since God has ordained that the faculties of knowing and willing should find enlightenment through the senses, we cannot allow the person who is retarded to subsist at his lowest level. There is a vital challenge to help expand the functioning of the soul, even through an impaired organism. The child care worker meets a challenge: to help each youngster put his limited share into the furthering of God's creative work, to help him organize his restricted world, to develop the understanding of which he is capable, and to acquire knowledge of God that will lead him to respond with love to an all-loving Father.

A developmentally disabled person can learn to be orderly, punctual, and industrious. The good habits formed in such persons will help to compensate for their lack of judgment. Spiritual guidance can help the individual to see God in all things and to perform all his deeds with love for God. An individual with normal reasoning power may readily detect God's infinite love, but through habits of selfishness might let that love go unrequited. How many contributions in the field of literature, art or science are produced for mercenary reasons rather than for the purpose of God's glory? And yet all creation is meant to contribute to the honor of God, the Source and Creator of all that is good.

Provision for continuous growth in spirituality is especially significant for adults who are developmentally disabled. Because they are adults, they should be met on an adult level, not as perpetual children. An adult approach includes reflection on Holy Scripture, especially the Gospel stories and prayer experiences. Faith community implies the sharing of joyful occasions and concern for those who are in sorrow. Days of prayer or a weekend retreat culminates careful preparation. Spiritual direction for adults with developmental disability enables them "to deepen their faith through recognition and clarification of God's all-abiding presence in their lives . . . to increase their love by becoming personally aware of sin, limitation and weakness that interferes with loving relationships . . . to strengthen their hope through uniting their sufferings with the sufferings of Jesus . . ." as experienced by Sister Joyanne Mueller who piloted a spiritual direction program for adult residents at St. Coletta School.

All persons are here on earth to glorify God and to work out their own salvation. All, even the most disabled, must direct their efforts to that end. The fullest expression of life is to love and serve God, the Creator of life, and this is possible for developmentally disabled persons. Their limited contributions may never gain human recognition, yet they are in some way exerting a positive influence on the lives of others. Frequently people are amazed to observe the attentive kindness of individuals, who themselves are handicapped, toward aged or crippled persons. In certain instances a whole family has been brought into closer relation with God through the example and influence of a member who is developmentally disabled and at the same time an inspiring example of caring for others.

Another role of the mentally underprivileged is to offer to more gifted persons an opportunity for charity which, in its truest sense, is the motivating force of all human greatness. The secret lies in recognizing that God has created some people to give service to those less fortunate. Our attitude toward Christ's "little ones" is our attitude toward Him.

Sharing, creating, and loving predominate among human satisfactions. Love, particularly, is the most powerful of incentives and enters in some manner into all that we achieve. Persons who have so little to share or to give, who lack great creative ability and whose love remains on the level of a child, can be a stimulus for the creativeness and truly devoted charity of more highly endowed individuals. If all people were sufficient to themselves, what outlet could love find?

A spiritual challenge to persons who are developmentally disabled is found in the sacraments of the Church. These sacraments provide milestones in their lives. Baptism welcomes an individual into the family of God. Special preparation for the sacraments offers teachable moments in explaining the fullness of Christian life. Readiness for Holy Communion underscores communication with God. Union with each other in the Christian family is enriched through union with Jesus in Holy Communion. Sister Kathryn Jennings explains:

> In this bond of fellowship all that each member does, or fails to do, vitally affects the community. As goodness builds it up and strengthens each member, so sin, a refusal to love, breaks down and weakens the bonds of mutual support. As sin distances us from God and from commu-

nity so the Sacrament of Penance brings us back rejoicing to the forgiving arms of our Father and of one another, to experience the fullness of life within the Eucharistic community which is the Church.

Because reconciliation brings peace and joy, celebration of this sacrament should be a joyous occasion. The new Rite of Penance allows for a personal encounter with the confessor which can be supportive and comforting to the person seeking reconciliation. Guidance in the expression of sorrow for saying "No" to Jesus, and encouragement in the promise to give a "Yes" response through improved behavior, helps the child, the adolescent or the adult to grow in a way of life that is pleasing to Jesus. This growth and desire form a preparation for receiving Jesus in Holy Communion.

Coming of the Holy Spirit is personalized in the sacrament of Confirmation. A simplified profession of faith renews the baptismal promises. Depending upon the level of understanding, instruction is an appropriate preparation for Confirmation. Some individuals will always lack the understanding needed for this preparation but should be privileged to have the sacrament administered at an appropriate age. Sister Coletta Dunn asserts:

> Post-Confirmation instruction seems to be an important need for retarded youth. When we recall their inability to read like their normal peers, we perceive the value of additional instruction as we introduce them to Christian adulthood. Sometimes the confirmant's sponsor can become teacher and advocate. At other times he can find welcome in religious, educational and recreational activities tailored to his needs.
>
> If we take Confirmation and post-Confirmation instruction seriously, handicapped youth will know that the Church cares. They and their parents will read the signs of

an accepting Church. All—the handicapped, their families and the religion teachers—will grow spiritually and socially from the Confirmation experience. (NAMR/Spring 1976)

The sacrament of the Anointing of the Sick should not frighten with the thought that death is near. Elderly people who are developmentally disabled and those who are sick find the Church ready to sustain them with this anointing. The sacrament offers a time of prayer when family members and faithful friends gather to pray, with the priest, for healing of the body or for peace of heart during the final moments of life.

Death is the fact of life's termination that each person must face. Complete honesty is a qualification for assisting the child or adult when death approaches. Any questions asked by the individual who is developmentally disabled call for an honest answer. The person dealing with one who is facing death must be comfortable with the thought of this final moment. A firm faith in God's goodness and confidence in His personal love for each human person are strong supports in helping the child or adult whose death is near. Death can be compared to a new birth. Just as the unborn child has no consciousness of all that life holds forth, so the person facing death cannot visualize all the joy and beauty God has prepared for those who respond to His love.

The person who is developmentally disabled can be helped to understand that in eternal life there is freedom from every handicap. Perfect joy replaces the mental and physical sufferings that accompany disability and are intensified by infirmity. The Anointing of the Sick prepares the individual to accept death with confident love and trust. This sacrament offers a communal experience when Christian people intercede for the sick person, confidently expectant of renewed health or that the person will be raised to a new life in Christ.

The *Pastoral Statement of the U.S. Catholic Bishops on Handicapped People* reminds us that Jesus in His ministry frequently associated with persons who were "forced to live on the fringe of society.... Our interaction with them can and should be an affirmation of our faith.... We are one flock that follows a single shepherd."

Although many individuals are so limited that others must take responsibility for them all through life, they help in their own way to make the world a better place. They serve as a sounding board for the society in which we live. "The greatness of a civilization can be measured by the provision it makes for its least members," as Cardinal Cushing stated. In reviewing the history of mental retardation we will see that, with the dawn of Christianity, a new era loomed for people who are handicapped.

Currently active in this new era is the National Apostolate with Mentally Retarded Persons (NAMRP), an organization devoted to promotion of full membership in the Church for persons with developmental disability. NAMRP emphasizes the human dignity of persons who are mentally retarded. The growing attitude among members is that they minister *with* persons who are handicapped rather than giving service to or for them. In its steady growth NAMRP witnesses that persons who are mentally retarded not only exemplify Christian values but can stimulate and call forth the commitment of all people concerned with their welfare.

11 *Historical Survey*

A natural question arises as more people become aware of the condition currently known as developmental disability. Frequently the questions are asked: "When was this condition first recognized? When did developmental disability become a common problem?"

The existence of children with mental retardation was generally unknown several generations ago. Unless the problem struck home, with someone in the family affected, most people neither knew nor cared about individuals who did not progress at the expected rate of development. Often they were hidden away in their own homes, victims of the confusion due to lack of knowledge about mental retardation, or developmental disability.

Now those of us who work in the area of special education usually find, in the course of a conversation, that persons we meet are aware that the child of a relative, or perhaps of a friend or business associate, is developmentally disabled. Eagerness for information indicates a widespread interest in those individuals whose mental growth has not kept pace with their physical age.

The Therapeutic Papyrus of Thebes, inscribed at about 1500 B.C. and discovered in 1862 A.D., refers briefly to mental "debility." In the early ages only the most severe and deformed types of mental deficiency were recognized. Mild forms of developmental disability, identified as presenting problems in our complex civilization, did not interfere with the simple life patterns of primitive people. Those less fortunate because of deformity or profound retardation were generally derided in public, treated with aversion in their own homes, ridiculed and persecuted abroad. The term "idiot" was linked with a curse of the ancient gods, leading to forfeiture of human rights and privileges. Treatment reflected horror and disgust.

Survival of the fittest played a strong role in the philosophy of some ancient societies. In an inhuman attempt to preserve the integrity of the race, infants who could be indentified as mentally deficient and those with physical deformity were allowed to perish. The Spartans sought prowess for their battles with the Athenians. Infants who were weak and feeble of mind or body were thrown from a cliff or left to perish on the hills or in deep caves. Infanticide was also practiced in Athens and in Rome.

The young mother of today on her hospital bed, torn between the desire to take her newborn infant home, although diagnosed as developmentally disabled, and the urge to save later pain of separation by immediate placement in a state hospital, might well compare herself with the mothers in ancient Rome. Cicero intimates that the father had power of life or death over a child. He could protect the pride of the family when a defective infant was placed at his feet. Children with handicaps who escaped the paternal death sentence endured a life of ridicule and scorn, were sometimes mutilated to become more effective beggars, were sold into slavery, or might become pitiable objects of amusement in the houses of the idle rich and the Roman nobles. Seneca's wife had a blind imbecile as her pet. Sometimes by a freak of fortune, an individual who lacked the balance of normal intelligence would reach a high position. Nero in the first century A.D., Commodus in the second, and Elegabalus in the third, each wielded tyrannical power without benefit of intelligent thought.

The ancient Persian prophet Zoroaster counseled tender care for the mentally weak. Confucius, the great philosopher of China who lived about five hundred years before the birth of Christ, showed similar solicitude. To the Mohammedans, the Koran gives this special charge: "Give not unto those who are weak of understanding the substance which God has appointed you to preserve for them, but maintain them thereout, clothe them, and speak kindly unto them."

With the spread of Christianity another era dawned for those who were afflicted by mental or physical defect. Jesus taught a new way of life—one based on love and mercy. He who would not break a bruised reed nor quench the smoking flax was so kind and gentle that He attracted children, and none of them was rebuffed. St. Paul, in his Second Letter to the Thessalonians, exhorted the Christians to comfort those who were weak of mind.

About three hundred years later, St. Nicholas, the bishop of Myra, provided care and protection for persons whose minds were those of children. Euphrasia, from the court of Emperor Theodosius, entered a convent to take up the work of caring for idiots and imbeciles who were dependent on charity. No attention was given in the early centuries to higher grades of mental retardation such as are now differentiated by mental test techniques. Only those who were severely retarded were identified for special care.

In 600 A.D. a beautiful Irish princess named Dymphna fled from her own father. Death rather than loss of innocence made St. Dymphna a patroness of the family care program at Gheel, Belgium. In the late nineteenth century other European countries adopted similar programs of family care for persons who were mentally deficient.

Also associated with the care of children who are developmentally disabled is St. Coletta, born in Corbie, France, in 1381. Her mother was sixty years old at the time of Coletta's birth. The aging parents had prayed to St. Nicholas that they might have a child. When their petition was granted, they named the baby Nicoletta in honor of the good saint who excelled the modern Santa Claus in his love for children.

Nicoletta was better known by the abbreviated name Coletta. As a young girl she did not grow well but was content with her stature until she heard her father say that he was sorry to have so stunted a child. At this moment, although she was not dwarfed in mental growth, Coletta experienced the pain of feeling different from the average or normal. Concerned over the grief of her parents, Coletta took the problem to God in prayer and visited a shrine of the Blessed Mother.

In answer to her prayer, Coletta grew tall, with surpassing beauty and poise. This remarkable "adding to stature" will probably not be repeated in the lives of modern children who are mentally retarded. God's ways are not ours, but His providence responds to the prayer of faith. Coletta's kindness to the afflicted points to the fact that various modern programs for developmentally disabled persons are conducted under the patronage of this medieval Franciscan saint.

During the Middle Ages numerous dwarfs who were mentally defective lived in the castles of nobility. This may cause surprise unless we recognize that midgets in present-day programs are remarkable for winsomeness of personality. Where they are accepted and loved, they give joy to those about them. Some who were grotesque appeared in circuses, even as they do today. Others played with the royal children or became jesters in the courts of kings. Centuries later some of these similarly attractive, intriguing little people found their way to St. Coletta School.

Little Betsy, for example, supervised me with motherly solicitude all the time I was her teacher. On a cold winter morning she would chirp warmly, "How many times have I told you to keep that shawl close around you?" She would try to pull tighter the edges when she could hardly reach them. One tiny little chap, on the day of his admission, said, "I think it's only fair to tell you that I know karate." His threatening gestures didn't scare anyone and he is now so happily adjusted that he no longer resorts to them.

These engaging little people remind us of medieval France where they were looked upon as "infants of the good God," and their homes were considered blessed. The attitude toward these children was one of such reverence that they were protected from harm and shielded from many dangers of which they were unaware. Sometimes, through alms received, they were the support of the family. In many parts of Europe and the Orient persons who were mentally deficient wandered without fear until the attitude of reverence gave way to superstition and later to persecution. So-called reformers spread the idea that evil spirits possessed those individuals who were mentally weak or demented. Severe beatings and other forms of punishment were supposed to drive out Satan. The age of Christian kindness became submerged in an era of whips and chains.

New hope came in the middle of the seventeenth century when St. Vincent de Paul began his ministry of Christlike charity. In an old chateau that had belonged to Anne of Austria, queen to Louis XIII and mother of Louis XIV of France, Vincent gathered abandoned children whom he picked up on the streets during the night. Among them he found little ones who were developmentally disabled.

The industrial revolution in eighteenth century England involved a cruel dependence on child labor. Employers were coerced to accept one child who was mentally deficient with a group of about twenty pauper children. In the rigorous factory system only the strongest and most able could survive the long hours of tedious labor.

Also in the eighteenth century, Jean Jacques Rousseau carefully distinguished the child from a miniature adult. He made the child, not the subject matter, the center of interest in education. This step pointed toward the period of enlightened care for children with mental retardation, although Rousseau himself refused to work with any child who was feeble or sickly. "Let another tend this weakling for me; I am quite willing, I approve this charity, but I myself have no gift for such a task," Rousseau is quoted as stating.

France justly deserves recognition as the birthplace of special education because of an experiment by Jean-Marc Gaspard Itard (1774–1838) in training the senses to stimulate responses of the mind. Itard was foremost among several dedicated, sensitive and talented persons in the nineteenth century who opened new vistas for individuals who were mentally retarded. In his experiment Itard found that if the reflective power in a person of low mentality is awakened by stimulation of the senses, further development can be expected.

Itard's contribution to learning concerned a wild boy caught in the woods of Aveyron, France, by a party of hunters. Itard was eager to attempt educating this boy, about twelve years of age, whom he called Victor. To him it seemed that the boy merely lacked training. Victor had developed animal-like characteristics. Food was selected by smell and he did not relish the meals of civilized people. To take a drink he would lie flat upon the ground and immerse his chin in water. Victor walked on hands and feet, tore off garments, and constantly tried to escape. He fought with his teeth, but seemed pleased when petted or caressed. Signs of intelligence were few. He did respond to the sound of the letter "O" or the word "Oh," but Victor had no articulate language. Although his life span reached into the forties, he lacked the power of speech. His ear, attuned to the sound of a falling nut, failed to respond to human words.

This savage lad from Aveyron presents the first recorded example of a wild boy reclaimed from the life of animal existence. Determined to remove the figurative mark of the beast from the forehead of this human being, Itard diligently entered upon his self-imposed task. However, in spite of Itard's ingenuity, Victor's progress was painfully slow. He became violent when frustrated by new demands and continuous efforts.

The principles Itard developed were similar to those applied in our own day when working with individuals who are severely retarded. First of all, Itard tried to interest the boy in civilized living by making it more pleasant than his previous existence in the forest of Aveyron. Second, because Victor failed to respond to ordinary sensation, Itard stimulated his nervous sensibility by strong, contrasting sensory experiences. Third, he attempted to extend Victor's range of ideas by developing new needs to replace his primitive wants. Since the boy did not talk, Itard's fourth principle aimed at inducing Victor to speak by making speech absolutely necessary to fulfill his needs. Itard's final principle concerned the objects of Victor's own interest and encouraged human contacts. He tried to persuade the boy to apply simple thought processes such as might be expected of a young child.

With profound interest in his pupil, Itard worked untiringly. In his own estimation the results were disappointing. Itard began to recognize that Victor was mentally defective rather than an uncivilized human being of normal intelligence. He tried to modify his methods accordingly. When Itard finally realized that the boy was grossly devoid of intelligence, he abandoned further hope of helping him. Bitterly disappointed, Itard exclaimed: "Unfortunate! Since my pains are lost and my efforts are fruitless, take yourself back to your forest. . . ." Victor was cared for during his remaining years by Madame Guerin, a maternal housekeeper, until he died in her home in 1828.

Itard failed to note the improvement in Victor although

the boy had not become mentally normal. To appreciate the true worth of Itard's efforts, he needed to compare the wild boy of three years before with the ever-so-slightly improved individual after his attempt. A similar comparison holds true in our present-day efforts to educate individuals who are severely retarded. The person working most closely with the child may fail to see progress or, if the goal is set too high, may be disappointed at failure to meet the objective.

Frequently a person who does not work intimately with the child who is developmentally disabled has a better perspective for observing progress. This was true of Itard's student, Edouard Seguin (1812–1888). Seguin watched the efforts of his master with great interest and saw what Itard failed to appreciate: the improvement that had gradually taken place. This observation prompted Seguin to systematize Itard's views and to adapt them to the treatment of persons with mental defect. From this beginning Seguin proceeded to develop his physiological method which spread to all countries.

Seguin, with keen intelligence and a power of original thinking, was well qualified for the task he attempted. Unlike Itard, he did not try to "cure," or make normal. Seguin faced the problem of minds defective in functioning and endeavored to bring them a few steps forward, raising low mental ability to a somewhat higher plane. Vivid sense impressions, carefully regulated activity, and limited choices allowing for quick detection of error were techniques he used. Seguin made short steps significant and strengthened the power of choice. Impaired nervous systems responded favorably to these methods.

Seguin, a lover of children, realized that much could be accomplished through love and a certain element of freedom. More fully than did Itard, Seguin understood that persons considered to be "devoid of understanding and heart" did possess some degree of responsiveness. This limited power, if awakened, could be exercised. Seguin studied the individual and adapted activities to his need and level of ability, a key to success in working with pupils who are mentally retarded. His methods consisted almost entirely in training first the hand and then involving all the sense organs, gradually leading toward development of ideas and a grasp of moral principles.

In his 1983 book, *A History of Mental Retardation,* Scheerenberger presents this summary:

> Seguin's theory of education and its application was encompassing, ranging from passive exercises for the non-ambulatory child through academic training and vocational placement for the more capable individual. His curriculum was quite contemporary to nature: learning involved perception, imitation, coordination, memory, and generalization.... In essence, the moral aspects of education involved developing, whenever possible, a strong sense of values, obedience and participation, duty, and responsibility for work. Education without the moral component was unacceptable.

In 1848 Seguin came to the United States and assisted in founding the early state institutions in Massachusetts, New York, and Pennsylvania for care and treatment of children who were developmentally disabled.

Somewhat before this time, in 1836, a young physician from Zurich, Johann Jakob Guggenbuhl, spent his vacation in the valleys of Switzerland. His sympathy was aroused when he saw a deformed cretin dwarf praying before a wayside shrine. Cretinism, a condition due to lack of thyroid and leading to stunted growth, was common in the area. Dr. Guggenbuhl resolved to devote his life to improving conditions for cretins in the Swiss valleys.

With only his sympathy as a guide, Guggenbuhl determined to found a hospital where systematized care could be given. He obtained a site on the Abendberg, about four thousand feet above sea level. Cretinism was unknown at this lofty height.

Dr. Guggenbuhl used methods similar to those of Seguin. Lessons adapted to the special needs of the cretin proceeded from the training of the muscular system to education of the senses, development of ideas, and a grasp of moral principles. A simple diet consisting mainly of vegetables, fruit, milk and bread contributed to a marked physical improvement. Transporting cretin children at an early age to the higher purer atmosphere seemed to awaken mental powers. Free life in the open air was combined with the stimulation of baths, massage, and exercise. Nature's miracle of beauty at these lofty heights had an exhilarating effect on individuals from valleys so shaded by mountains that sunlight seldom reached them.

For a time Guggenbuhl's project on the Abendberg brought him fame with its apparent success. Visitors from Europe and America expressed enthusiasm by returning to build institutions in their own countries. They invited Dr. Guggenbuhl to visit and encourage the workers. Heralded as an apostle of the unfortunate, he traveled from place to place. The success at Abendberg reached a peak in the 1850's and then the tide turned.

Too much had been promised and too much was expected. Certain individuals with apparent cures were paraded for a time. Envy and suspicion replaced admiration for Dr. Guggenbuhl. Neglect and abuses crept in during his absences. Almost overnight he became a tragic figure. The Abendberg closed and Guggenbuhl died in 1863, broken with grief.

All of us who are engaged in work with children and adults who are developmentally disabled must be realistic in what we claim to do. The question might be asked, "How many can you cure?" We do not promise to cure. With true mental deficiency we can only assist the individual to develop limited intelligence to the optimum level. When retardation is due to a physical cause, as lack of thyroid in a cretin, improvement follows upon effective treatment early in life.

Maria Montessori (1870–1952), an Italian educator whose methods are receiving international recognition, developed teaching techniques based on the ideas of Seguin. She stressed individual aptitude, multiple-sensory learning, and the acquiring of knowledge through using specially prepared, self-corrective learning devices. A graduate in medicine, Dr. Montessori worked for a time with a group of children whom she referred to as idiots but taught so successfully that some of these youngsters were able to take a public school examination in reading and writing with mentally normal children of the same age, and to pass it successfully.

Dr. Montessori believed that children have a strong sense of personal dignity, that they like order, repetition, freedom of choice, work rather than play, with silence and a surprising ability to concentrate when absorbed in a task. She tried to give them independence in caring for their own needs, such as washing, dressing, and eating. In her kindergarten the children learned lessons referred to as "Exercises in Practical Life." A second area of attention centered about the development and refinement of sensory powers and perceptions, particularly of touch, sight and hearing. Third, and perhaps Montessori's greatest contribution to education, was the "Didactic Apparatus" or "Materials for Development." These materials were presented after a child had mastered the sensory training.

The Montessori learning apparatus helped the young child acquire basic elements of the tool subject. Her methods spread to countries throughout the world but were opposed in the United States by John Dewey's philosophy of permissive education. Since the late 1950's Montessori schools include classes for normal and gifted children. Methods used to self-educate these youngsters are based on principles and materials first used by Montessori with children who had learning deficiencies. At her death in 1952 in Noordwijk, Holland, Montessori's reputation as an educator was well established.

In the middle of the nineteenth century a number of private schools in Europe had demonstrated that children with developmental disability were no longer objects of charity, pity, or even abuse: they could be taught! Hopeful enthusiasts claimed that, given adequate opportunity, they were capable of learning, that some could be cured in this way, and that others could advance toward normalcy. These ideas developed and transferred to America.

The United States maintained the principle of educating all children at public expense but had no provision for those who were mentally retarded. To provide a similar opportunity for those with mental handicap as was already available for normal children, the first state school was established in 1847 at Waverly, Massachusetts. Plans provided that children would return to their homes after a few years of special training brought their defective intelligence to a normal level. Admission to the state school and retention there were limited to the school age period.

In 1850 the prevailing thought was that training increased intelligence, rather than simply providing skills and information. A distinction was soon made, however, between individuals who were merely trainable and those who were considered educable. Accurate classification came at a much later date. Since the purpose of the early state institutions was to prepare for normal living, there was strenuous objection to admitting any individuals who were considered uneducable. At this time there was no plan for custodial care by the state, no provision for children with the lowest levels of intelligence.

After the first state school was founded, others followed in quick succession. By 1875 they were increasing at the rate of one school every three years. Already there were long waiting lists. The public saw a need for more institutions but failed to supply adequate funds. Evidence proved that a few years of special training did not raise subnormal intelligence to an average level. Since many of the children admitted seemed unable to respond to the program, state schools came to be regarded as "asylums for incurables" rather than as centers of special training. Only a small number had improved to a point where they were able to return to the community, attempting to meet the requirements of normal citizens. Now the objective aimed to achieve improvement within limits of the child's potential rather than striving for complete normalcy.

State schools next began training pupils for permanent residence in the institutional environment. This was a natural step, and applied to those who could function only as sheltered helpers. In these institutions there were daily tasks in the kitchen, dining room, dormitories, laundry, garden, or on the farm. These types of work gave purposeful occupation and proved an economical means of helping to maintain the school or institution while insuring a lifetime home for the residents.

A program of industrial training in useful skills was introduced for those who qualified. Skill became a substitute for abstract intelligence and shops formed an essential part of the institution. There was an objection, however, because parents had not forgotten the original purpose for which state schools were founded. To these parents, industrial training meant putting residents to work for the benefit of the institution. Many people objected to their sons or daughters being assigned jobs on the school premises. They were unaware of the total picture of mental retardation, its extent, its costliness, and the social problems involved. Gradually the idea of protecting society as well as helping the individual was accepted.

Institutions developed more rapidly as the dream of cure was abandoned. Through the years thousands of children who were mentally retarded had been under observation. Many who returned to their homes after a lengthy period of training had not adjusted successfully. Improvement of habits and acquiring of skills, even the undoubted increase in mental age, did not equal normalcy.

When the theory of protecting society had taken hold, parents no longer objected to shop work and industrial training in the institutions. With this impetus production soon exceeded institutional needs and selling of products began. Outside industry objected on the grounds of unfair competition. This disapproval brought an end to the possibility of self-support through industry within the institutions.

Special classes, opportunity rooms, or individual progress classes in the regular graded schools have a history of purpose similar to that of the state institutions. The original objective was restoration to normal school placement by special training in the basic school subjects. Failing to accomplish this purpose, the program shifted in emphasis to handwork. Stress was on information and skills that would be useful after leaving the school.

During this period more adequate surveys were taken. The results doubled and tripled previous estimates of the number of children who required special education. Several states enacted laws for sterilization of girls who were mentally deficient. Thousands of them were subjected to this process without solving the problem.

By 1925 most states had one or more institutions although permanent segregation was no longer considered necessary or feasible. The idea of guardianship within the community had developed and also a new system within the institution itself: the colony plan. Dr. Charles Bernstein, Rome State School, New York, promoted this plan. I enjoyed the interesting experience of observing it in action during a summer workshop for teachers in special education.

The plan functioned on various levels. Young children

went to school at their colony home, usually a large residence under the supervision of a married couple. Older boys and girls lived at a colony but were employed in the neighborhood. Some worked in private homes, others in factories, restaurants, or on farms. This plan offered challenge as a wage earner while allowing more freedom than the regimentation common to institutional living. Responsibility leading to independent living motivated the young workers. Actually, the success of the colonies can best be estimated in human values: the building of character through new hope and opportunity.

The colony plan reduced costs to the state and relieved crowding in the institutions. Economic conditions following World War I favored the rise of the colony system, but when the great depression took its toll the colonies showed decline. Self-support for persons who are developmentally disabled depends upon favorable employment conditions in general.

The idea of a parole system, or community supervision, came from Europe. America introduced state-controlled supervision in the community. Families were compensated for taking care of the patient to avoid danger of exploitation. Their source of income depended upon satisfactory care and good behavior was the price of freedom from institutional living for the individual.

Current thinking maintains that no person who is developmentally disabled should remain in an institution if satisfactory adjustment at home or in the community is possible. Foster home placement is an alternative providing more emotional satisfaction than is found in a crowded institution. Sheltered workshops offer variation to the daily schedule, but are dependent upon the need for products in an age when automation is rapidly replacing hand labor.

A movement which swept the country resulted in organization of parents who have children with developmental disability. Soon after 1930 the first small, local Parent Groups

center for a three-week period helped one young man to understand that he was risking his job by drinking. The employer cooperated by holding the position open to give an otherwise promising employee a second chance.

In a treatment program for offenders who are developmentally disabled, "habilitation" is a preferable term to describe the process. "Rehabilitation," frequently used, means restoring the person to a previous level of acceptable social values and behavior. Habilitation takes the individual as he is and guides him toward improved levels of independence based upon values, behavior, knowledge and skills. Cooperative effort is needed to draw a developmentally disabled person from criminal involvement to reach the optimum level of acceptable behavior in a self-supporting situation.

One questions how much habilitation can take place in a prison setting. Lack of understanding, lack of funding, and lack of individual caring in overcrowded areas of confinement result in sacrificing goals that would be realistic for developmentally disabled persons. The criminal justice system needs to reach out beyond present limitations. Only then can adaptive behavior deficits be overcome by consistent programs of habilitation.

In her research study, *A Different Drummer,* Theresa Johanek says:

> Mental retardation need not be seen as a lifetime sentence of stupidity and impaired functioning.... More recently legal and civil rights advocates have added their voices and applied the power of litigation in response to the cries of direct service personnel, concerned professionals, and citizen advocates. The combined effort is beginning to have profound effect not only in the field of corrections but also on the entire criminal justice system.

were formed. The effect was gratifying. These people understood each other and their problems. Parents, who previously felt that they were alone in bearing a burden which grieved and shamed them, now found that other good citizens had been concealing similar problems. The relief of mutual unburdening gave freedom for a new outlook. These parents began to exert influence for helping their children on a community basis. They worked to educate themselves and the public to the needs of children with mental retardation.

In the history of parent groups, 1950 marks the formation of a national organization. This momentous step united eighty-eight local groups, operating independently in various parts of the country, under the title "Parents and Friends of Retarded Children." In 1952 the name was changed to the "National Association for Retarded Children," popularly known as the NARC. In 1980 it assumed the title "Association for Retarded Citizens" of the United States.

The ARC strives to improve the general welfare of all persons with mental retardation. While local units give parents the satisfaction of doing something directly for their loved ones, the national organization achieves great forward movements through the strength of an ever increasing membership. This expansion, under expert leadership, includes people of all professions. The aid which they are able to give to each other and to citizens with developmental disability is beyond measure. The ARC has improved social attitudes toward persons who are retarded, developed acceptance, fostered recognition of the need for accurate diagnosis, supported legislation, and promoted effective treatment based upon current research.

12   *Breakthroughs*

Parent movements leading to organization on a national level in 1950 formed a breakthrough of historic importance. Parents, more than anyone else, can dramatically and realistically describe their own problems in meeting the needs of children and adults who are developmentally disabled. Federal and state legislators take notice when they hear parents say, "My son or my daughter has a right to share in the educational privileges of a democracy." The first major breakthrough in recognition of human and civil rights for citizens who are developmentally disabled, and increased federal funding for special programs and human services, has been largely due to parental influence.

Parents themselves needed to come out of the shadows so that children in need of special services could benefit. Accurate referral to sources of genuine help and current information relieves some of the tension they feel. Parents of a child who is developmentally disabled can assist other parents who may be as near as the next door neighbor. Together they can alert the public to the fact that this is a problem for *all* society, not just for families directly concerned.

Among parent groups it is inspiring to know that some parents join the organizations for children with mental retardation, not because they have a child who needs this program, but from a sincere desire to help those who do have a handicapped child. "If I can do nothing more than offer another lap for a helpless child to sit on . . ." confided one woman who joined parents in their attempt to bring stimulation into the daily routine of children in an institution.

An advantage of belonging to parent groups is growth in mutual understanding. Difficulties are discussed; needs are recognized; ideas are suggested; friendships are formed. Parents who are weighed down by their burden may come to realize, through first-hand contact, that their son or daughter is not the most afflicted. They also learn to recognize that each individual, although handicapped, has redeeming qualities. Parents who are inclined to think that their child is superior to other children with mental retardation benefit by seeing these other children as viewed by their parents.

The mere satisfaction of sharing with other people who have lived through a similar experience often relieves tension. The understanding developed between parents will dispel much of the heartache expressed by a mother who wrote, "Why must people be stamped as disgraceful because of this disability in one of their children?"

Parents with a family member who is developmentally disabled are somewhat inclined to look for and remember incidents which are painful to them. They can help themselves by developing a less sensitive, more objective attitude. Thus they will realize that in many people there is a goodness which compensates for the unkindness of those who are critical. Frequently it is the hurt or the insult which lingers in the parents' memory, while the little kindnesses to them and their child may be forgotten.

To cherish an appreciation for the goodness of other people, capitalizing on its smallest manifestation and watching for its growth, is excellent mental hygiene. Often we find in people what we seek. Keeping a friendly, hopeful attitude may eliminate some of the heartaches and plant the seeds for a better future based on understanding and insight.

Thoughtful parents see their child as a family responsibility and realize that the fact of developmental disability does not excuse them from their duty toward a family member.

Unless emphasis is placed upon giving the individual every opportunity to grow and take responsibility when possible, the parents will be overwhelmed, unhappy, enmeshed in confusion. John W. Melcher says, "Each child born in our society should have the benefits of our accumulated knowledge and be treated with attention given to each of his or her civil and moral rights as granted by laws of the land and God." (Unpublished ms., February 1983)

When they band together and use existing forces to the best advantage, parents become a dynamic force. Instead of laboring under the conviction that the government or other agencies should carry full responsibility for children with mental retardation, parents can work with these sources, offer their support and experience, and share in the planning process. Service on committees whenever possible will enable them to effect changes that will improve facilities and provide a more individualized program of treatment for the future of children and youth who are developmentally disabled.

The impact of parent organizations is monumental. This explosion of parent interest brought about a transition from people who, early in the century, were expected to be docile and uninformed, to a dynamic force today. Their impetus toward developing legislation, through specific concerns and lobbying efforts, has affected the entire field of special education. The initiative and support of parent organizations help to guarantee due process and assurance of civil rights for persons who are developmentally disabled. Because they are personally involved, parents can accomplish these objectives.

Parents celebrate the growth in public awareness of problems involving mental retardation. They foresee a day when characteristics of certain types of developmental disability, such as Down's syndrome, for instance, may be remediated. Programs of early intervention offer great hope. Sister Joanne Marie Kliebhan, foundress and director of the St. Francis

Children's Activity and Achievement Center, Cardinal Stritch College, Milwaukee, writes:

> Ever since Kirk (1958) demonstrated the educability of the retarded in preschool years, society has slowly moved from a negative "put them away and forget them" stance to a much more positive "reach them and work with them as early as possible" attitude.
>
> Research has shown that the period before language develops is one of the most critical phases of human development. Basic motor skills are established, the ground work for perceptual development is practically completed, and the roots of cognitive development are laid down. In the case of retarded, learning impaired, or developmentally delayed children, early intervention is even more critical in order to "short circuit" the acquisition of necessary life skills and to help these youngsters become as competent, fulfilled, and independent as possible.
>
> The development of successful early intervention programs for the handicapped requires the participation not only of special education but of virtually every discipline and profession. But the ultimate success of these programs depends upon the understanding and participation of parents and families who, during infancy and the early years, are the primary teachers of intervention strategies.
>
> Combining all of these essential components into a model early intervention program, the St. Francis Children's Activity and Achievement Center was established in 1969. Committed to the philosophy that "all children can learn if we can learn how to teach them," prescriptive learning assignments are programmed and supervised for each infant and toddler enrolled in the Center program geared to the child's individual level and rate of development. Diagnostic services and multi-disciplinary therapies are available at the Center for wide varieties and levels of learning problems.

> The Infant/Toddler program at St. Francis CAAC has focused primarily on Down's syndrome children because of their rate of incidence and their recognizable symptoms at birth. However, other infants suffering from spina bifida, hydrocephaly, cerebral palsy, and other physical anomalies are served at St. Francis as well. Beginning as early as two months of age, the infant and the infant's family receive professional help through home and Center-based programming. Following the initial intake evaluation attended by an Infant/Toddler Development Specialist, a Physical Therapist, Occupational Therapist, Vision Therapist, Speech (Feeding) Pathologist, and the Parents, the child's developmental level and needs are assessed and an appropriate treatment plan is outlined. Services are begun immediately and the child's progress is continually monitored and recorded.
>
> These early intervention strategies are enabling retarded children to develop a level of movement skills far beyond expectation . . . to attain speech and language skills appropriate for their chronological age . . . to reach academic levels before unprecedented . . . and above all, to develop healthy, positive self-concepts, and a rewarding sense of achievement.
>
> Building on these foundation stones, continuing education and therapy can enable the retarded child to reach the maximum of his or her individual learning potential. (Personal communication to the author)

For all areas of special need a major breakthrough appeared in 1962. President John F. Kennedy's Panel on Mental Retardation published its report to the President, entitled, *A Proposed Program for National Action to Combat Mental Retardation.* This intensive study by a wide range of experts generated immediate interest. With emphasis on urgency of action, John F. Kennedy accelerated progress during his remaining year of presidency.

President Kennedy called attention to the neglect of persons who are mentally disabled which evaded American standards of compassion and human dignity. All agencies, public and private, were called upon to confer the full benefits of our nation on those who suffer from mental disabilities. Research for prevention and remediation were strongly stressed.

One of the most remarkable changes was in attitude. Parents no longer needed to feel ostracized because their child was mentally retarded. An accident that could happen in the family of the President of the United States could happen without disgrace in other families. Physicians became less prone to prevail upon parents to railroad a newborn child with signs of abnormality into a state hospital and then try to forget its existence.

Greater sensitivity also developed in regard to terminology. Archaic terms that were degrading to developmentally disabled individuals could no longer be tolerated among caring persons. The use of labels was frowned upon, although not discarded because they seem to serve a purpose in getting services needed for individuals who are developmentally disabled.

I was privileged to be present for the First International Awards of The Joseph P. Kennedy, Jr. Foundation, Washington, D.C., December 6, 1962. I saw the urgency and strategy with which a dedicated President encouraged research, service and leadership by professional and lay people in America and throughout the world. The awards aimed to stimulate young scientists, and especially medical students, to direct their efforts toward the field of mental retardation:

> The Foundation extends a warm welcome to the 120 medical students from the thirty-eight medical schools on the Eastern seaboard whose professors and deans selected them to attend the International Awards dinner and the

scientific meetings of the National Institutes of Health. They are the outstanding members of their classes and we are proud to have them among us. We hope that these students and their colleagues have found some stimulation here. Perhaps some of them may even be inspired to explore the intricacies of the field of mental retardation a little more fully on their own. It would be a service and blessing if this were so, for it may well be the light of their promise that brightens the future of millions of families and their children, those born and those yet to be. (Program of International Awards, 1962)

The awards also called attention to the value of research efforts in other areas related to mental retardation. Motivation for more personnel with better qualifications for care and treatment of persons with developmental disability, also for increased civic leadership concerned with the welfare of these persons, was richly provided.

With this impetus from the President of the United States, recommendations of the Panel moved into action. Emphasis was on research, preventive and remedial measures, programs of special education, clinical and social services, methods and facilities for improvement of care, a new legal and social concept including protection of civil rights for mentally disabled persons, provision of manpower through increase of adequate training programs, and provision for growth in public awareness. Results are far reaching, intangible, difficult to measure, but a strong element of growth became continuous with activation of the Panel's recommendations.

International Awards bestowed by The Joseph P. Kennedy, Jr. Foundation during ensuing years continued to recognize outstanding research, service and leadership. Legislation indicated a positive response during the decades that followed. Major federal agencies administered programs of funding that reached into the areas of education, vocational training, employment, social security benefits, and a general recognition of the rights of persons who are developmentally disabled. In 1968 the International League of Societies for the Mentally Handicapped drafted a "Declaration of General and Special Rights of the Mentally Retarded" which was adopted in 1971 by the United Nations General Assembly. The seven articles of the declaration decreed:

> **Article I**—The mentally retarded person has the same basic rights as other citizens of the same country and same age.
>
> **Article II**—The mentally retarded person has a right to proper medical care and physical restoration and to such education, training, habilitation, and guidance as will enable him to develop his ability and potential to the fullest possible extent, no matter how severe the degree of his disability. No mentally handicapped person should be deprived of such services by reason of the costs involved.
>
> **Article III**—The mentally retarded person has a right to economic security and to a decent standard of living. He has a right to productive work or to other meaningful occupation.
>
> **Article IV**—The mentally retarded person has a right to live with his own family or with foster parents, to participate in all aspects of community life, and to be provided with appropriate leisure time activities. If care in an institution becomes necessary, it should be in surroundings and other circumstances as close to normal living as possible.
>
> **Article V**—The mentally retarded person has a right to a qualified guardian when this is required to protect his

personal well-being and interest. No person rendering direct services to the mentally retarded [person] should also serve as his guardian.

Article VI—The mentally retarded person has a right to protection from exploitation, abuse and degrading treatment. If accused, he has a right to a fair trial with full recognition being given to his degree of responsibility.

Article VII—Some mentally retarded persons may be unable, due to the severity of their handicap, to exercise for themselves all of their rights in a meaningful way. For others, modifications of some or all of these rights is appropriate. The procedure used for modification or denial of rights must contain proper legal safeguards against every form of abuse, must be based on an evaluation of the social capability of the mentally retarded person by qualified experts, and must be subject to periodic reviews and to the right of appeal to higher authorities. (United Nations, 1971)

These carefully delineated rights raised the concept of the mentally retarded individual as a person. Further development was the recognition that every individual, regardless of severity of handicap, has some potential for growth. Each one is a person, deserving of respect, and of the care, treatment and training that will enhance his/her limited endowment of human qualities.

Harvey A. Stevens, in *The 8th Harry A. Waisman Memorial Lecture,* states:

> The struggle for human rights is much more than our government's foreign policies or the cry of the politically oppressed in far off countries. It is here—in our neighborhoods—our cities—and our rural areas. It is among us when we oppose the disabled living as our neighbors. It is

here when we find it difficult to include them in the daily activities of our communities—when we establish separate church services and scout troops for them—when we mistakenly classify many black and chicano children as retarded, or show indifference to them—or when we submit them to educational processes and environments far beyond their ability to comprehend or cope.

Adults who are developmentally disabled are among those whose rights have been most neglected. Programs for those of adult age who spent their early years at home require careful planning and the provision of appropriate facilities. It is most important that parents give their child [adult] assurance of care after they are gone. When a parent dies there is great anxiety on the part of a son or daughter who is developmentally disabled unless there has been a precise explanation of the provision made. "Who will take care of me now?" expresses this concern.

A system of interlocking services to meet various needs of semi-independent adults in a family-like environment could help to ease this concern. These adults are individuals with different personalities and a variety of needs that a single program does not satisfy. An element of choice is needed for aging persons to replace the home care options their parents gave them during earlier years. An overwhelming desire of these parents is to see the family member who is handicapped happy and secure in a homelike residence with warmth of supervision, respect for privacy, and individualized attention to spiritual, physical, emotional and social needs. Answering this description is the resident worker program at St. Coletta School offering sheltered employment, attractive living arrangements, peer companionship, and involvement in the wider community.

A forward-looking plan developed for the Alverno Cottages at St. Coletta School provides a model program for men and women with developmental disability who are moving into the final decades of life. This elderly population benefits by choices of program that are stimulating to each individual while sharing the companionship of friends. To describe the program:

> The Alverno Study Committee has considered the present physical, emotional, social, spiritual and educational enrichment needs of the older adult who is mentally handicapped.... The residents uniformly confirmed their expectations that Alverno would continue to be their home. They expressed hopes to have continuing opportunities for choice in sports, task oriented responsibilities, spiritual growth, crafts, and family involvement. As the result of these interviews and on-site observations, we have tried to anticipate how improvements in the facilities and programmatic opportunities will develop unrecognized or untapped potentials of the handicapped aging adult....
>
> We believe the development of exciting, innovative programs will utilize potentials of these people not yet developed.... These new creative services will provide learning experiences for professionals and students seeking comprehensive training in the care of the aging handicapped adult. This will further the pioneering philosophy of St. Coletta School which has provided growth experiences throughout the life span of mentally handicapped persons....
>
> Recommendations for a wide variety of specific activities are made to provide for current and future needs of older individuals with regard to spiritual, social, physical, educational and cultural development.... The Committee has kept in mind futuristic orientation which includes

possibilities for respite care, continuation and augmentation of existing day-care services, and a cottage concept to provide options for homelike living.

All activity and living areas must be wheelchair and limited ambulation accessible. All program areas must have adequate material acquisition and storage areas. All remodeled and newly constructed areas must be designed and executed in manner so that as homelike an environment as possible can be created for the residents.

Another breakthrough has occurred with the concept of normalization. This concept does not imply a forced normalcy onto a person who is developmentally disabled. Rather, it refers to an attempt to have a normal rhythm of the day, freedom from useless structures and restrictions, so that persons who are retarded can live under conditions and with patterns of life as close as possible to the average mainstream of society.

A normal rhythm of the year, with holidays, vacations, and events of personal significance to the family, should be arranged to include the member who is handicapped. Activities appropriate to age will ward off childishness humiliating to an adult whose preferences should be respected. Normalization of peer groups includes both sexes in situations and activities where ordinary citizens would mingle in society. The least restrictive, most productive and enabling environment helps the person who is handicapped to reach a maximum level of independence. Mainstreaming tends to enable students with learning problems to be a part of the regular stream of education. Since life for the most part will be lived among normal people, mainstreaming keeps the school age child with developmental disabilities in this group.

With the trend toward deinstitutionalization, and children who are handicapped living at home and attending local schools, mainstreaming is a natural result. The efficacy of special classes have been weighed against the normalizing experience: being part of the regular class. This can be an ideal situation, or it can mean that the child with mental retardation is more segregated than when grouped with other pupils who have learning problems.

Although Public Law 94-142 does not mention mainstreaming, it has become a reality for many children with developmental disabilities. Improved self-concept is a positive result when acceptance and learning conditions are favorable. An important consideration involves the preparation of regular classroom teachers to meet the needs of special pupils while coping with accountability to the class as a whole. Concern for individual differences allied to favorable attitudes toward children with handicaps enables school personnel to set a climate of acceptance in the classroom.

The philosophy of mainstreaming prescribes that as many children as possible—even if physically, mentally or emotionally handicapped—should be included in the regular classroom but with supportive help from resource personnel. Childhood is a once-only experience, with all influences having far-reaching effects. Life-streaming, rather than mainstreaming, might be the more descriptive term because the whole future of the individual is affected by early experiences so crucial to the child who is developmentally disabled.

The mainstream does confront a handicapped child with unique needs; here educators face many challenges while also meeting the needs of more gifted pupils who have a right to optimum development. Some children with handicaps will benefit more by a new start in a special class or a residential school where an accepting environment and flexibility of program opens up whatever wells of strength the child possesses. The choice between mainstream or special placement must be made on a child by child basis.

Choices rest with accountability not only of teachers but of the total educational system. Accountability presents crucial issues often overlooked in the past. Responsibility toward a society that supports educational programs calls for a share in setting goals and accountability toward reaching these goals.

The general trend toward deinstitutionalization is a positive breakthrough but it does increase the need for responsibility on the local level. The community must be ready and willing to accept persons who are developmentally disabled as they strive to live a new kind of life. If the local climate is cold and suspicious, former residents of institutions may find themselves more segregated, but in a different way, than when confined to a large-group living situation. Neighborhoods can welcome, but they can also reject, the resident of a family-like group home. Terrible loneliness gnaws at any hope of success in self-support when young people who are developmentally disabled find themselves rejected by people who should be neighbors in spirit as well as in location. There are examples of remarkable success when these residents are recognized as persons with a purpose in life. Like all other people, they have only one life to live and it should be lived at the optimum level of contentment for self and contribution to others.

What is best for the disabled member needs to be kept in balance with what is best for the family as a whole. This unit needs to be preserved and sometimes it must be at the cost of seeking residential placement for a member who is handicapped. In those situations where institutional placement is necessary for the care of a severely disabled child, possibly because of ill health of the mother or in order to preserve normal family living, there should be freedom from feelings of guilt. Where there are small, family-like institutions with adequate patient care, decisions of this kind are less painful.

A need for advocacy for handicapped persons is gradually

making way for self-advocacy. Too often disabled persons are rated by what they can't do rather than by what they can accomplish. In one way they need to "sell themselves," but, on the other hand, their self-concept usually depends upon what other people think of them; their successes are measured by the expectations set for them by those who are important in their lives.

Kevin Patrick Tracy, perhaps best known of former students of St. Coletta School, is recognized internationally for promoting self-advocacy. Kevin came to St. Coletta's at age six and remained until he had completed the vocational habilitation program. Then, while employed at Cardinal Stritch College, Milwaukee, Kevin became editor of *The Milwaukee Citizen,* the nation's first newspaper for and by citizens who are developmentally disabled. He currently edits a similar paper in Texas where he is now located. Kevin began this aspect of his career as cub reporter for *St. Coletta Homelights* and later became its most prolific reporter. In a recent interview Kevin commended his teachers and group parents at St. Coletta's for having taught him to think for himself and for encouraging him to use his talents to the best of his ability.

Kevin is presently Coordinator of Self-Advocacy, Association for Retarded Citizens, Austin, Texas. He is himself a prime example of independence and self-actualization as he travels the country lecturing on self-advocacy. Kevin was keynote speaker at the International League of Societies for Persons with Mental Handicaps at the 8th World Conference, Kenyatta International Conference Centre, Nairobi, Kenya, November 25, 1982. He also headed a panel of self-advocate consumers. Kevin's text speaks for himself and his peers in the self-advocacy movement. Some excerpts are:

> We want to be known as persons first; our handicaps should be secondary. My personal belief is that organiza-

tions both national and international ... must first and foremost recognize that mentally handicapped people are equal partners with their fellow human beings.... In the words of Pope John Paul II, "A mentally handicapped person is one of us, a sharer in the same humanity."

It is not enough that international organizations promote and secure the rights of persons who are mentally handicapped. These organizations must also provide every opportunity for handicapped persons to fully integrate into their organizational structure as equal partners. They must work to encourage and provide opportunities for people who are mentally handicapped to make decisions in programs and services that will affect their lives. The International League, and other groups like it, must understand that people who are mentally handicapped are their own best advocates in recognizing their rights and needs to lead a normal life to the best of their ability.

Individuals began organizing with other handicapped persons into self-advocacy groups, so that as a group they could have a strong voice in making their feelings and needs known in the communities where they live. This movement first started in Sweden in the 1960's and spread to other European countries. In the early 1970's it spread across the Atlantic Ocean to the United States and Canada. I am very proud to say that my country, the United States of America, has been one of the leaders in the development of the self-advocacy movement....

Some groups provide direct services to their membership, such as counselling centers, and training workshops which train people to be more independent. Organizing adult education classes to teach their members basic skills and publishing informative newsletters are among some of the services these groups offer their members. Some groups offer a social outlet for their members ... organize parties, dances, and arrange package tours.... Many groups have a formal organizational structure which includes a constitution and by-laws or charters, elected officers and board of directors and statewide organizational structure. Whatever method is used, these groups have a common purpose, the desire to be their own advocates. These groups are saying, "We *can* and we want to speak for ourselves and make decisions for ourselves...."

I would like to stress the importance for parents, professionals and self-advocates to work as a team, to be in partnership. Being in partnership, to me, means equal participation between people who share the same rights and responsibilities.... You must go one step further in that partnership. You must try to put yourself in their place to truly understand their wants, needs, desires and opinions. There is an old American Indian saying, "You cannot really know a man, unless you have walked a mile in his moccasins."

To be in partnership with persons who are handicapped, parents and professionals must be willing to communicate on equal terms with these people. A mentally handicapped person knows when someone is treating him as an equal or when he is being "talked down" to or being patronized.... If parents and professionals are ever to understand the concept of self-advocacy, they must understand that for many years persons who are mentally handicapped have often been made to feel less than human, without dignity or self-respect.... One of the best examples I have read about personal dignity is the story of "The Elephant Man," the life of John Merrick. Here was a man who, because of his physical handicaps, suffered every indignity human beings could inflict upon another. Yet John Merrick never lost his dignity. One of the best illustrations of this is when he returned from France to England. At the London train station he was beset by an angry mob of people who ridiculed him. He cried out, "I am not an animal; I am a human being!"

I believe that self-advocates, in their own way, are saying the same words: "I am a human being!" Mentally handicapped persons individually, and as groups, are stat-

> ing to their fellow citizens that they want dignity and human rights. We are saying that we are capable of leading full and productive lives to the best of our ability....
>
> So let us here today rededicate ourselves to working for the rights and dignity of all citizens of the world who are mentally handicapped. Let us have a true partnership made up of parents, professionals and self-advocates which will reinforce to the whole world the self-advocates' belief that "We are human beings. We want to be treated with dignity and respect."

Self-advocacy develops a rapport among peers; handicapped persons gain experience and discover inner resources as they come to the aid of others who are in some way disabled. The self-advocate speaks to the need of equal educational and appropriate employment situations. Advocacy activities involve opportunities to emphasize what the individual is able to do, rather than his inefficiencies.

Public awareness grows with positive examples, such as that of Kevin Patrick Tracy, in the need of developmentally disabled persons to speak for themselves. Within their own areas of influence, they can move into openings for leadership, as Kevin has done.

The trend for self-advocacy moves naturally into consideration of the "Decade of the Disabled," proclaimed by the United Nations Assembly for the years 1983–1992. A unanimous resolution adopted a World Program of Action for Disabled Persons, a companion resolution to that proclaiming the Decade of Disabled Persons. According to United Nations estimates, as many as five hundred thousand disabled persons worldwide may benefit by these initiatives.

Governments, international and national organizations are urged to provide leadership for people everywhere to promote participation of disabled persons in national and community affairs. The National Office on Disability, a private non-profit organization, was formed in January 1982 as a direct outgrowth of the International Year of Disabled Persons. The Board of Directors includes disabled and non-disabled leaders from all sectors of American life. Through the Community Partnership Program, awareness is promoted, information is disseminated on programs and issues, partnership is advocated and private sector initiative is encouraged. The National Office on Disability supports local committees of disabled and non-disabled volunteers striving to improve attitudes toward people who are disabled, to expand access to public places, to promote greater opportunities in education, housing, employment, transportation and recreation, and also to take preventive measures toward disabling conditions. (LINKS, November 1982; National Association of Private Residential Facilities for the Mentally Retarded)

What will be the breakthroughs as we look ahead to the year 2000? William V. Schipper and Leonard A. Kenowitz did a Delphi study (1975), gathering opinions from leaders in the field and compiling the data under this title: *Special Education Futures: A Forecast of Events Affecting the Education of Exceptional Children: 1975-2000.* According to the authors, "The rationale for the Delphi is that projections of the future are largely based on personal expectations of knowledgeable individuals."

As we move through the 1980's such events as due process procedures, inclusion of special education courses in teacher training programs, parent involvement and mainstreaming are already in process. Some states require continuing education for all teachers as a basis for annual renewal of certification. Within the 1980's locator systems and appropriate counseling services for "high risk" parents are advocated.

Sixty percent of the nation's public school teachers are expected to practice prescriptive, individualized teaching by 1987, according to this study.

The zero reject concept in effect nationwide and school calendars adapt the hours in the day and the days in the year to the handicapped by 1990. Also programs and support services for persons profoundly retarded are indicated as an integral part of the public school system. Ombudsmen will be employed to protect the rights of children who are developmentally disabled and of their parents. Private schools for children who are handicapped will have to meet collaboratively developed national and state accrediting standards. In some states the educable mentally retarded will no longer be classified as children who are handicapped. Basic concepts of medicine and principles of drug-induced behavior modification will be included in the pre-service training of special educators.

Equal educational opportunities for the handicapped among various states are predicted for 1995; also almost total access to public communication via technology such as television for the blind and deaf, telephone for the deaf, and newspapers for the blind. Innovative rapid transit systems and worldwide travel for persons who are handicapped are predicted for the year 2000. A Federal "Peace Budget" should replace the traditional "Defense (War) Budget."

Other predictions for the year 2000 suggest that remote rural school systems will utilize the helicopter for pupil transportation. State supported residential educational programs for persons who are deaf, severely retarded and multiply handicapped will be almost non-existent nationwide but, according to the study by Schipper and Kenowitz, the federal government will fund one hundred percent of the cost of education for children who are handicapped.

The fulfillment of predictions rests on personal leadership and on the providence of God, but planning to include persons who are handicapped in all possible social milieus will, in the light of this study, "fulfill the promise of a brighter future" for children, youth and adults who are in some way developmentally disabled. There is a challenge for the members of society to become more fully human persons so that they can accept —even welcome—those who differ from theoretically established norms. As Jean Vanier explains:

> They cannot be persons of ambition and action in society and so they develop a capacity for friendship rather than efficiency. Persons who are handicapped can in this way breach an opening in the walls which we of the twentieth century have built around ourselves through fear of others.... The greatest suffering of the person who is mentally handicapped is to feel different, unwanted, unloved, useless. He needs friends who will help him to discover his own place in society, friends who will love and respect him. (Notes from talks of Jean Vanier)

Families in the future are challenged to allow for the element of risk in the lives of members with developmental disabilities. In the past many of these individuals have been deprived of their opportunity to reach full potential because parents feared the risk. Allowing for choice, and taking the risk that comes with the right to choose, calls for willingness to listen, and then to be enablers for persons with developmental disabilities as they strive to reach goals chosen for themselves. These persons have a right to their share of happiness and self-realization as citizens of this world, and to strive for the eternal happiness God has promised to those who love Him.

Annotated Bibliography

In selecting this bibliography I kept the parent particularly in mind, but with the realization that the parent may be a professional person. I have also been mindful of the fact that teachers, doctors, clergymen, and other specialized persons are manifesting a timely interest in the problems relating to developmental disability.

Since I have refrained from using footnotes, this bibliography will indicate sources of material, and will be of special value to students who wish to do further and more scientific reading.

The future for children who are developmentally disabled rests with their peer groups—the boys and girls of today. I am listing a *Youth Bibliography* also, to help acquaint these young people with facts and characteristics relating to mental retardation. The selections range from picture stories with unnumbered pages for the youngest readers to more advanced books for maturing adolescents. To derive mutual benefit, parents and children may share the reading of these books and discuss points of interest.

Baker, Bruce L., Seltzer, Gary B., & Seltzer, Marsha Mailick. *As Close as Possible: Community Residences for Retarded Adults,* Boston: Little Brown & Company, 1974. 265 pp. A descriptive study of the existing types of programs that grew up in response to the movement toward alternatives to isolated and overcrowded state institutions; the book is an outgrowth of a nationwide study to examine community-based facilities.

Balthazar, Earl E., & Stevens, Harvey A. *The Emotionally Disturbed, Mentally Retarded: A Historical and Contemporary Perspective,* Englewood Cliffs, N.J: Prentice-Hall, Inc., 1975. 333 pp. The authors emphasize the role of emotional stress in causing personality disturbance as well as the emotional factors associated with mental retardation. Information on differential diagnosis and treatment is included.

Baskin, Barbara H., & Harris, Karen H. *Notes from a Different Drummer,* New York: Bowker Company, 1977. 375 pp. A guide to juvenile fiction portraying handicapped persons; explanatory chapters are followed by summaries and analyses of books for children and youth, thus forming an annotated guide to juvenile readings related to various handicapping conditions.

Bernardin, Joseph L. Cardinal. *Let the Children Come to Me,* Cincinnati: St. Anthony Messenger Press, 1976. 58 pp. Illustrated guide for parents and teachers in the religious instruction of children.

Blackwell, Marian Willard. *Care of the Mentally Retarded,* Boston: Little Brown & Company, 1979. 489 pp. Treats full spectrum of mental retardation with special implications for persons in the nursing profession.

Bissonnier, Henri (Translation by S. Carolyn Frederick, O.S.F.). *The Pedagogy of Resurrection,* New York: Paulist Press, 1979. 225 pp. Deals with the religious formation and Christian education of persons who are handicapped or maladjusted.

Blatt, Burton. *In and Out of Mental Retardation,* Baltimore: University Park Press, 1981. 369 pp. These "Essays on Educability, Disability, and Human Policy" are a plea for better understanding, greater compassion, and more effective means of providing real life for persons who are mentally retarded.

Bogdan, Robert, & Taylor, Steven J. *Inside Out: The Social Meaning of Mental Retardation,* Toronto: University of Toronto Press, 1982. 232 pp. The approach is a breakthrough; interviews permit two persons, labeled as mentally retarded, to tell their own stories from which conclusions are drawn.

Brown, Bertram & Courtless, Thomas F. *The Mentally Retarded Offender,* Washington, D.C.: National Institute of Mental

Health, Center for Studies of Crime and Delinquency, Government Printing Office, 1971. Research pertinent to the incidence of mental retardation in relation to the criminal justice system.

Browning, Philip L. (editor), *Rehabilitation and the Retarded Offender,* Springfield, IL: Charles C. Thomas, Publisher, 1976. 349 pp. Contributors to this volume bring together a complex body of knowledge dealing with a much neglected topic. The record of spontaneous discussions by experts concerned with the retarded offender is included.

Buth, Lenore. *Sexuality: God's Precious Gift to Parents and Children,* St. Louis, MO: Concordia Publishing House, 1982. 142 pp. Book six of the New Concordia Sex Education Series: designed for adults to help them deal with their own sexuality from a Christian point of view. Illustrated.

Carson, Mary. *A Guide for Friends, Neighbors and Relatives of Retarded Children,* Chicago: Claretian Publications, 1977. 64 pp. Prologue by Rita Dranginis; this little book offers guidance toward acceptance and an understanding attitude to the parents as well as to children who are mentally retarded.

Cegelka, Patricia T., & Prehm, Herbert J. *Mental Retardation: From Categories to People,* Columbus, OH: Charles E. Merrill Publishing Company, 1982. 419 pp. Comprehensive text book, well organized to cover a wide range of topics relating to mental retardation with emphasis on human aspects.

Cullen, Rev. Patrick P. *An Investigation of the Attitudes of Normal Siblings and of Parents Toward Their Mentally Retarded Family Member,* Milwaukee, WI: Unpublished Dissertation, Cardinal Stritch College, 1975. 99 pp. Compares relationship of attitudes to provide for all families a better understanding of how to cope with a family member who is retarded.

Davis, Sister Deborah. *Religious Experience and Profoundly Developmentally Disabled Persons,* Milwaukee, WI: Unpublished Research Paper, Cardinal Stritch College, 1982. 62 pp. The challenge to teach all children to know and love God includes the severely and profoundly disabled, with strong belief in the mystery of God and his power to touch the hearts of these individuals.

Dougan, Terrell, Isbel, Lyn, & Vyas, Patricia (compilers). *We Have Been There,* (Salt Lake City, UT: Lithographed by Publishers Press, 1979; New edition, Abingdon Press, 1983. 283 pp. Parents and siblings speak out in a guidebook for parents of people with mental retardation.

Drew, Clifford J., Hardman, Michael L., & Bluhm, Harry P. *Mental Retardation: Social and Educational Perspectives,* St. Louis, MO: The C.V. Mosby Company, 1977. 247 pp. Perspectives on important issues are presented by competent contributors.

Egg, Maria. *The Different Child Grows Up,* New York: The John Day Company, 1969; Distributed by Steck Vaughn Company, P.O. Box 2028, Austin, Texas 78767. 128 pp. A guide in dealing with the problems of adolescents and adults who are mentally retarded.

Gaulke, Earl H. (editor). *Concordia Sex Education Series,* St. Louis, MO: Concordia Publishing House, 1982. A complete Christian sex education program—from preschooler to parent—for use in the home; an audio-visual presentation with text books and study guides.

Geren, Katherine. *Complete Special Education Handbook,* West Nyack, New York: Parker Publishing Co., Inc., 1979. 267 pp. A comprehensive handbook with contents ranging from rights of students who are handicapped to information on current federal rules and regulations; helpful in setting up and operating a successful special education program.

Grossman, Frances Kaplan. *Brothers and Sisters of Retarded Children,* New York: Syracuse University Press, 1972. 249 pp. A study of the siblings of retarded children and how they are affected by a family member who is developmentally disabled.

Haavik, Sarah F., & Menninger, Karl A. *Sexuality, Law, and the Developmentally Disabled Person,* Baltimore: Paul H. Brookes Publishing Co., 1981. 191 pp. Deals with the complicated issues surrounding the needs and experiences of individuals who are mentally retarded when they undertake the roles of marital partners and parenthood, living as sexual persons.

Hall, Suzaane E. (editor). *Into the Christian Community,* Washington, D.C.: National Catholic Educational Association, 1982.

115 pp. A religious education guidebook for professionals and para-professionals working with disabled persons in parishes, schools and institutions based on contributions by experienced leaders.

Haskett, Sister Sheila. *Director's Handbook for Journey with Jesus,* Milwaukee, WI: Cardinal Stritch College, 1977. 162 pp. Description of program and guide for the teaching of Special Religious Education based on experience in setting up and conducting successful programs.

———, Dunn, Sister Coletta, *et al., Journey with Jesus, Gospel Study,* Milwaukee, WI: Cardinal Stritch College, 1978. 276 pp. A religion curriculum carefully planned to meet the needs of adults who are developmentally disabled.

Howell, Kenneth W., Kaplan, Joseph S., & O'Connell, Christine V., *Evaluating Exceptional Children: A Task Analysis Approach,* Columbus, OH: Charles E. Merrill Publishing Co., 1979. 284 pp. Special edcuation has come a long way from its basic interest in the severely handicapped; by moving into the area of the mildly handicapped, special education has been forced to come to grips with subtle issues.

Jennings, Sister Kathryn. *Reconciliation and the Developmentally Disabled Child,* Unpublished Research Paper, Cardinal Stritch College, Milwaukee, WI, 1977. 118 pp. This study investigates growth in a sense of community in children who are developmentally disabled. The process combines prayerful catechesis and celebration of reconciliation on both the readiness level and the preparation level for the sacrament of penance, culminating in the celebration of reconciliation and assessment of subjects' responses to evaluation activities.

Johanek, Theresa Bernadette. *"A Different Drummer": The Mentally Retarded in the Criminal Justice System,* Milwaukee, WI: Unpublished Research Paper, Cardinal Stritch College, 1981. 126 pp. This essay reaches out to help make known and provide for the unmet human needs of offenders who are mentally retarded.

Jordan, Thomas E. *The Mentally Retarded* (Fourth Edition), Columbus, OH: Charles E. Merrill Publishing Co., 1976. 734 pp. This comprehensive textbook has been consistently updated and is a helpful reference for dealing with many aspects of mental retardation.

Knight, David. *The Good News About Sex,* Cincinnati: St. Anthony Messenger Press, 1979. 312 pp. An optimistic, spiritually oriented presentation on sex and its role in life.

Kucera, Sister Shirley. *A Comparison of Attitude Change in Normal Siblings of Developmentally Disabled Persons through Informational Talks or by Working Informally with Developmentally Disabled Persons,* Milwaukee, WI: Unpublished Dissertation, Cardinal Stritch College, 1976. 92 pp. This study explores attitudes of normal siblings toward a developmentally disabled family member and the possibility of changes in these attitudes.

Kushner, Harold S. *When Bad Things Happen to Good People,* New York: Schocken Books, 1981. 149 pp. A father who has seen his afflicted son suffer and die shares with other parents in similar circumstances.

Leman, Paul. *Deinstitutionalization: A Cross-Problem Analysis,* Washington, D.C.: Department of Health and Human Services, 1980. 119 pp. This monograph focuses on the inter-relationships among individuals in need of special care, their families, and the state; indicates that normalization ideals can help toward the establishment of higher quality, non-traditional alternatives to replace older patterns of institutionalization.

Lyons, Charles M. "Due Process and Children with Special Needs." *The Journal for Special Educators,* Spring 1981, New York: 179 Sierra Vista Lane, Valley Cottage, 10989. pp. 244–249. JFSE keeps abreast of latest happenings in the broad field of special education.

Moxley, David, Nevil, Nevalyn, & Edmonson, Barbara. *Socialization Games for Mentally Retarded Adolescents and Adults,* Springfield, IL: Charles C. Thomas, Publisher, 1981. 118 pp. The authors provide a practical framework for encouraging positive social behavior in group situations through use of games that appeal to individuals who are developmentally disabled. Group leadership is explained and seventy socialization games are included.

National Committee for Human Sexuality Education. *Education in*

Human Sexuality for Christians, Washington, D.C.: United States Catholic Conference, 1981. 118 pp. Intended for persons responsible for planning and giving instruction in sexuality; highest level of support from the Church to the idea and practice of education in human sexuality which respects Christian moral values.

Perske, Robert. *Hope for the Families.* Nashville, TN: Abingdon Press, 1973. 96 pp. Illustrations by Martha Perske. Subtitled, "New Directions for Parents of Persons with Retardation or Other Disabilities," an optimistic guide for parents as they face the unique challenge of providing a satisfying life for the child with developmental disabilities.

———. *New Life in the Neighborhood,* Nashville, TN: Abingdon Press, 1980. 77 pp. Illustrations by Martha Perske. The author explains "How Persons with Retardation or Other Disabilities Can Help Make a Good Community Better." Interesting, informative, practical.

President's Panel on Mental Retardation. *A Proposed Program for National Action To Combat Mental Retardation,* 1962. 201 pp. This program points the way to much of the progress which has influenced services for persons who are developmentally disabled during ensuing years.

Reinbold, Mary Rose. *The Handicapped Child and Intra-Familial Relationships,* Milwaukee, WI: Unpublished Research Paper, Cardinal Stritch College, 1978. 41 pp. A review of research pertaining to the impact of the presence of a child who is handicapped on the family as a unit and also on the individual members.

Rollin, Henry R. *The Mentally Abnormal Offender and the Law,* New York: Pergamon Press, 1969. 139 pp. Presents an inquiry into the working of the relevant parts of the Mental Health Act, 1959; recommends panels of jurists and psychiatrists to work with offenders having mental problems.

Sapir, Selma G., & Wilson, Bernice. *A Professional's Guide to Working with the Learning Disabled Child,* New York: Brunner/Mazel, Publishers, 1978. 239 pp. Includes information on the development of life plans, not just school plans, and examines basic considerations in planning alternative programs for children who are handicapped.

Shellock, Brother Boniface. *Educational Background Civil Servants Have When Dealing with Retarded Public Offenders,* Milwaukee, WI: Unpublished Research Paper, Cardinal Stritch College, 1980. 36 pp. Emphasis is on the need for in-service training so that police officers, lawyers and judges will have professional knowledge in the area of mental retardation.

Scheerenberger, Richard C. *A History of Mental Retardation,* Baltimore, MD: Paul H. Brookes Publishing Co., 1983. 311 pp. A comprehensive history of mental retardation presented with painstaking detail, high interest and readability. Excellence as a textbook is enhanced by a carefully prepared study guide.

Schipper, William V., & Kenowitz, Leonard A. *Special Education Futures: A Forecast of Events Affecting the Education of Exceptional Children: 1975–2000,* Washington, D.C.: National Association of State Directors of Special Education, Inc., 1975. 23 pp. Futuristic study, using the Delphi method, with a grant from the U.S. Office of Education, Department of Health, Education and Welfare, but opinions expressed do not necessarily reflect the position or policy of the U.S. Office of Education and official endorsement should not be inferred.

Simpson, Richard L., *Conferencing Parents of Exceptional Children,* Rockville, MD: Aspen Systems Corporation, 1982. 376 pp. Comprehensive information for answering the questions parents are sure to ask. The book includes a chapter on legal and legislative considerations.

Theodore, Sister Mary (Hegeman). *The Challenge of the Retarded Child,* St. Meinrad, IN: Abbey Press, revised education, 1969. 192 pp. A sharing based on years of experience in working with children and adults who are developmentally disabled.

Vanier, Jean. *The Challenge of L'Arche,* Minneapolis, MN: Winston Press, 1981. 286 pp. Compiled from eighteen individuals who have worked with Jean Vanier. This book exemplifies the art of learning to live together, with introduction and conclusion by

Jean Vanier. Includes a 1981 listing of all L'Arche homes in various countries.

Wehman, Paul, & McLaughlin, Phillip J. *Program Development in Special Education,* New York: McGraw-Hill Book Co., 1981. 454 pp. Teachers and parents are urged to work as a team and continually track the child's gains in different skills; special consultants may include occupational and physical therapists, speech pathologists and audiologists.

────── et al. *Vocational Curriculum for Developmentally Disabled Persons,* Baltimore, MD: University Park Press, 1981. 203 pp. Includes a detailed sequence of work skills; based primarily on experience with moderately, severely, and profoundly disabled individuals in preparation for productive sheltered employment.

Ysseldyke, James E., & Algozzine, Bob. *Critical Issues in Special and Remedial Education,* Boston: Houghton Mifflin Company, 1982. 300 pp. Deals with issues from historic perspective and current practice.

Szymanski, Ludwik S., & Tanguay, Peter E. *Emotional Disorders of Mentally Retarded Persons,* Baltimore, MD: University Park Press, 1980. 287 pp. Serves as a guide in treating emotional disorders associated with mental handicap.

Youth Bibliography

Adams, Barbara. *Like It Is: Facts and Feelings about Handicaps from Kids Who Know,* New York: Walker and Company, 1979. 96 pp. Illustrated with photographs by James Stanfield. First person narratives give insight into various types of handicaps including developmental disabilities/mental retardation.

Ameiss, Bill, & Graver, Jane. *Lord of Life, Lord of Me,* St. Louis, MO: Concordia Publishing House, 1982. 120 pp. Book five in the New Concordia Sex Education Series; written for youth ages 14 and up, and for parents, teachers, and other significant adults who may want to discuss the book with them. Illustrated.

Anders, Rebecca. *A Look at Mental Retardation,* Minneapolis, MN: Lerner Publications Company, 1976. Illustrated with photographs by Maria S. Forrai; foreword by Muriel Humphrey. Stresses the importance of using well the intelligence one has, and the responsibility of the school.

Bimler, Richard. *The New You,* St. Louis, MO: Concordia Publishing House, 1982. 64 pp. Book four of the New Concordia Sex Education Series; written for young people 11–14 years; also of value to significant adults who may be instructing the boy or girl.

Bonham, Frank. *Mystery of the Fat Cat,* New York: Dutton, 1968. 160 pp. Illustrated by Alvin Smity. The novel has a contrived plot but does carry the message of good sibling relations; the hero who is mentally retarded portrays some aspects of a savant.

Bradbury, Biana. *Nancy and Her Johnny-O,* New York: Ives Washington, 1970. 150 pp. Problems common to families with a retarded member seem to cause undue stress; parental denial, pressures to institutionalize, sibling relations are delineated.

Brightman, Alan. *Like Me,* Boston: Little, Brown, and Company,

1976. The story of what it means to be retarded, told in words and pictures. Illustrated by the author.

Brown, Roy. *Escape the River,* New York: Seabury, 1972. 160 pp. A boy with brain damage becomes the responsibility of his adoptive brother when the parents' marriage begins to disintegrate; portrays the example of a compassionate and caring boy who feels his sibling is being abandoned by the parents.

Byars, Betsy. *The Summer of the Swans,* New York: Scholastic Book Services, 1970. 142 pp. Illustrated by Ted CoConis. The story of sibling love for a younger brother and a teenager's sense of responsibility toward him. Her experience with this child, retarded since the age of three because of high fever, is a maturing process for Sara and offers insights into mental retardation.

Capelan, Bo. *Bow Island,* translated by Sheila LaFarge. New York: Delacorte, 1968. 140 pp. The setting is in Scandinavia where Johan, aged 11 years, meets a young adult who is mentally retarded. Contrasts are drawn between caring individuals who are sensitive to the problems and the capabilities of a person who is handicapped, and the cruelty of another who taunts, mocks and tricks the young adult who is retarded.

Christopher, Matt. *Long Shot for Paul,* Boston: Little, Brown and Company, 1966. 151 pp. Illustrated by Peter Caddell. A boy with intellectual impairment gets sibling support but less acceptance by a peer group; the basketball coach is sympathetic. The book offers some valid information on mental retardation and reflects community attitudes toward a child who is retarded.

Cleaver, Vera & Bill. *Me Too,* Philadelphia: Lippincott, 1973. 158 pp. Twin girls, and one of them is mentally retarded. The other tries to share her gifts by becoming protector and tutor to her handicapped sister.

Clifton, Lucille. *My Friend Jacob,* New York: E. P. Dutton, 1980. Illustrated by Thomas DiGrazia. The story of two boys who are friends and who help each other, but one finds it harder to learn new things.

Crane, Caroline. *A Girl Like Tracy,* New York: David McKay Company, Inc., 1966. 186 pp. Tracy, at age nineteen and severely retarded, is pampered by her mother, searched for by her tired father when she slips away, and presents a burden of responsibility for her younger sister, Kathy. Finally Tracy receives help in a workshop offering the training she needs, and Kathy is free to live a normal life.

Doorly, Ruth K. *Our Jimmy,* Westwood, MA: Service Associates, Publishers of Literature and Materials in Special Education, 1967. Illustrated by Kenneth Boudreau. The book is dedicated to all those children who share in the family responsibility of understanding and helping a brother or sister who is mentally retarded; stresses the family spirit.

Fabyer, Nancy W. *Cathy at the Crossroads,* Philadelphia: Lippincott, 1962. 190 pp. Illustrated by Howard Simon. The story centers about a lonely, insecure child and the efforts of her stepmother to build a relationship but who has a retarded daughter. The characteristics of retardation as presented seem contrived.

Fassler, Jean. *One Little Girl,* New York: Behavioral Publications, Inc., 1969. Illustrated by M. Jane Smyth; expresses a mental health approach for the very young child while telling the story of Laurie who is slow in doing some things.

Friis-Baastad, Babbie. *Don't Take Teddy,* New York: Charles Scribner's Sons, 1967. 218 pp. An adventuresome story of a Norwegian boy and his severely retarded older brother; after many struggles he sees the need for a special school.

Garrigue, Sheila. *Between Friends,* Scarsdale, New York: Bradbury Press, 1978. 160 pp. Mental retardation, and some of the factors causing this condition, are explained in simple, clear terms as part of this lively story.

Graver, Jane. *How You Got To Be You,* St. Louis, MO: Concordia Publishing House, 1982. 60 pp. Book three of the New Concordia Sex Education Series; written for boys and girls ages 8–11, and for parents, teachers and other significant adults who may want to discuss the book with the child. Illustrated in color.

Greene, Carol. *Each One Specially,* St. Louis, MO: Concordia Publishing House, 1982. 30 pp. Book one of the New Concordia Sex Education Series; written for children of pre-school age to be used by parents and other significant grownups who will read the book to the child. Illustrated in color.

Hill, Margaret. *The Extra-Special Room,* Boston: Little, Brown and Company, 1962. 312 pp. A young teacher starts a special class in an old mountain town with all the trials due to lack of understanding and too many children for her to meet their individual needs. She keeps her sense of humor and her love for the children grows as the year progresses.

Hirsch, Karen. *My Sister,* Minneapolis, MN: Carolrhoda Books, 1977. Illustrations by Nancy Inderieden. A teacher writes about her sister with the hope of dispelling some of the fear and ignorance that surround the subject of mental retardation.

Hofstein, Sadie. *The Human Story,* Glenview, IL; Dallas, TX; Palo Alto, CA; Oakland, NJ; Tucker, GA: Scott, Foresman Company, 1977. 32 pp. Facts on birth, growth, and reproduction with explanations and illustrations.

Hummel, Ruth. *I Wonder Why,* St. Louis, MO: Concordia Publishing House, 1982. 32 pp. Book two of the New Concordia Sex Education Series; written for children ages 6–8, and for parents, teachers and other significant adults who will read the book with the child. Illustrated in color.

Klein, Gerda, with photographs by Norma Holt. *The Blue Rose,* New York: Lawrence Hill and Company, 1974. Jenny is compared to a "blue rose" because she is different, loved by her parents but having difficulties because of inappropriate behavior.

Krauss, Bob (editor). *An Exceptional View of Life,* Norfolk Island, Australia: Island Heritage Limited, 1977. 64 pp. The Easter Seal Story, written and illustrated by handicapped children who, with a helping hand, have earned pride in a job well done.

Larsen, Hanne. *Don't Forget Tom,* New York: A John Day Book, Thomas V. Crowell Company, 1974. Illustrated; tells the story of Tom, six years of age, who is mentally handicapped. Tom's story will help young readers to relate with a child who is different.

Little, Jean. *Take Wing,* Boston: Little, Brown and Company, 1968. 176 pp. A young girl takes responsibility for her seven-year-old brother because the parents seemingly ignore the fact that he is mentally retarded. Eventually James is referred for special education and Laurel is free to make friends of her own.

Magee, Catherine Fowler. *One of the Family,* New York: David McKay Company, Inc., 1964. 210 pp. A Down's syndrome baby is born the night his sister Sally graduates from high school. Early institutionalization is recommended. This troubles the family so they bring the baby home and Sally becomes his champion and an advocate for children who are mentally retarded.

Mayle, Peter. *"What's Happening to Me?"* Secaucus, NJ: Lyle Stuart, Inc., 1975. A guide to puberty with answers to questions the young person might be too embarrassed to ask.

———. *"Where Did I Come From?"* Secaucus, NJ: Lyle Stuart Inc., 1973. The facts of life in large print with illustrations by Arthur Robins.

Nixon, Joan Lowery. *Before You Were Born,* Huntington, IN: Our Sunday Visitor, Inc., 1980. Describes growth during the interuterine period; introduces role of God's love in the creation of a new person.

Ominsky, Elaine. *Jon O, A Special Boy,* Englewood Cliffs, NJ: Prentice-Hall, Inc., 1977. Photographs by Dennis Simonetti. Jon O has Down's syndrome. His story is told in words and pictures.

Perl, Lila. *Dumb Like Me, Olivia Potts,* New York: A Clarion Book; The Seabury Press, 1976. 181 pp. Olivia, who comes from a highly literate family, has reasons not to like school. Interest, humor, and suspense help to tell the story which shows that Olivia and a peer are rather smart girls after all.

Rinald, C.L. *Dark Dreams,* New York: Harper & Row, Publishers, 1974. 154 pp. A novel clearly depicting the persecution by a young mob of two persons who are mentally retarded. The story gives a presentation of the suffering involved for victims of false accusation (homosexuality) and by lack of toleration because of being different.

Smith, Gene. *The Hayburners,* New York: Delacorte Press, 1974. 64 pp. Illustrated by Ted Lewin; the story of a steer that is a loser, cared for, by a man who is mentally retarded, with a love that gains honorable mention for the steer. "Hayburner" is racetrack slang for a loser but the story has an encouraging message: with love and care even a hayburner can be a winner.

Stefanik, Alfred T. *Copycat Sam,* New York: Human Sciences Press, Inc., 1982. Illustrated by Laura Huff; a lesson for children and adults showing gradual growth in overcoming the hostility of an able child toward one who is given to imitation but lacks average ability.

Stein, Sara Bonnett. *About Handicaps,* New York: Walker & Company, 1974. 47 pp. An open family book for parents and children together with photography by Dick Frank; explores the relationship between two children, one of whom is handicapped.

———. *Making Babies,* New York: Walker and Company, 1974. 47 pp. A family book for parents and children to share; basic facts in large print.

Walker, Pamela. *Twyla,* Englewood Cliffs, NJ: Prentice-Hall, 1973. 125 pp. A girl of fifteen, mentally retarded, is killed in an automobile accident—the death might be intentional. The story is told in a series of letters giving detailed insights into her desires and frustrations, especially her longing to be loved.

Wartski, Maureen Crane. *My Brother Is Special,* Philadelphia: The Westminister Press, 1979. 153 pp. Noni explains that her brother is special; he is *not* weird.